PURE IN HEART

PURE IN HEART

DALLIN H. OAKS

BOOKCRAFT
Salt Lake City, Utah

Library of Congress Catalog Card Number: 87-73059
ISBN 0-88494-650-9

4th Printing, 1988

Printed in the United States of America

CONTENTS

PREFACE

This book explores the importance of motives, desires, and attitudes. It concentrates on thoughts rather than on actions.

Motives explain actions completed. Desires identify actions contemplated. Attitudes are the thought processes by which we evaluate our actions and experiences. Motives, desires, and attitudes are interdependent. All involve what the Apostle Paul called "the inner man" (Ephesians 3:16).

In describing the state of the inner man, the scriptures commonly use the word *heart*. This word occurs over a thousand times in the standard works, almost always as a figurative expression.

Heart is often used to identify the extent to which one is receptive to the message of the gospel. Nephi said, "The Lord . . . did visit me, and did soften my heart that I did believe" (1 Nephi 2:16). A later Nephi described his preaching to a people who "did harden their hearts and did not hearken unto the words of the Lord" (Helaman 10:13).

Heart is sometimes used as a synonym for *mind*. Speaking of the multitude who heard the risen Lord on this continent, the Book of Mormon says, "neither can the hearts of men conceive so great and marvelous things as we both saw and heard Jesus speak" (3 Nephi 17:17). "Their hearts were open and they did understand in their hearts the words which he prayed" (3 Nephi 19:33).

Heart is also used in contrast to *mind*, with *mind* apparently connoting the powers of reasoning (the intellectual) and *heart* connoting the powers of intuition (the spiritual). President Harold B. Lee used those two words in this contrasting sense when he said: "When we understand more than we know with our minds, when we understand with our hearts, then we know that the Spirit of the Lord is working upon us" (Harold B. Lee, *Stand Ye in Holy Places* [Salt Lake City: Deseret Book Co., 1974], p. 92).

Similarly, the Lord described the house of Israel as having "hardness of heart, and blindness of mind" (Ether 4:15). And at the beginning of his sermon, King Benjamin challenged his people: "Open your ears that ye may hear, and your hearts that ye may understand, and your minds that the mysteries of God may be unfolded to your view" (Mosiah 2:9).

As illustrated at length in this book, *heart* can also refer to motives, desires, and attitudes.

In the language of the scriptures, the word *heart* is a powerful figurative expression, rich in meaning. It is the primary instrument used to teach us that from the perspective of eternity and in terms of God's commandments the hidden thoughts of our minds are just as important as the observed actions of our bodies.

I hope this book will *encourage* those who feel deficient because they are unable to conform to the desired standard of visible action but whose invisible motives, desires, and attitudes are acceptable to God. I hope it will *challenge* those who feel self-satisfied with their visible and praiseworthy actions but whose motives, desires, or attitudes are not always appropriate.

Portions of this book are adapted from three of my talks. Chapters 3 and 7 are enlarged versions of sermons delivered in October general conference in 1984 and 1985 (*Ensign*, November 1984, pp. 12-14, and November 1985, pp. 61-63). Parts of chapters 1 and 4 were presented in a devotional address at Brigham Young University in October 1985 (*Ensign*, June 1986, pp. 64–67).

This book is a personal expression and is not an official statement of the doctrine of The Church of Jesus Christ of Latter-day Saints.

CHAPTER ONE

THE INNER MAN

"Who shall ascend into the hill of the Lord?" the Psalmist asked, "or who shall stand in his holy place? He that hath clean hands, and a pure heart" (Psalm 24:3-4). "I say unto you," Alma declared to his people, "can ye look up to God at that day with a pure heart and clean hands?" (Alma 5:19).

If we do righteous acts and refrain from evil acts, we have clean hands.

If we act for the right motives and if we refrain from forbidden desires and attitudes, we have pure hearts. Those who would "look up to God," those who would ascend and stand in the ultimate "holy place," must have "clean hands, *and* a pure heart."

It is easy to underestimate the importance of our motives, our desires, and our attitudes. The processes of our mind—what we sometimes call "the inner man"—are not visible to the eyes or susceptible to the other senses. As a result, we can slip into assuming that motives, desires, and attitudes are unimportant to our eternal welfare.

The scriptures and the living prophets teach otherwise. The Savior taught: "Blessed are the pure in heart: for they shall see God" (Matthew 5:8; 3 Nephi 12:8). The Book of Mormon prophet Jacob pronounced woe upon those "that are not pure in heart," saying they are "filthy this day before God" (Jacob 3:3). James characterized the importance of wholesome mental attitudes as well as correct actions when he proclaimed: "Draw nigh to God, and he will draw nigh to you. Cleanse your hands, ye sinners; and purify your hearts, ye double minded." (James 4:8.)

In one of his earliest sermons as President of the Church, President Ezra Taft Benson pleaded with Church members to make the changes in their personal lives necessary to "cleanse the inner vessel" ("Cleansing the Inner Vessel," *Ensign,* May 1986, p. 7).

Each time we partake of the sacrament we receive a powerful reminder of the importance of the inner vessel. Two of the three covenants we make in that sacred ordinance obligate our thoughts more directly than our actions. Those who partake of the sacrament witness "that they are willing to take upon them the name of thy Son," and "always remember him" (D&C 20:77, 79).

God has always commanded his children not only to reform their actions but also to purify their inner man. The commandments recorded in the Old Testament are mostly concerned with actions. Nevertheless, the Old Testament contains some powerful teachings addressed to what happens within the mind. The last of the Ten Commandments, "Thou shalt not covet" (Exodus 20:17), concerns desires and attitudes. Each of the three passages of scripture that are used in synagogue worship to express basic Jewish belief contains significant references to man's thoughts. (These are quoted below from a translation of

2

the Holy Scriptures according to the Masoretic text published 1962 by The Jewish Publication Society of America.)

> Hear, O Israel! The Lord is our God, the Lord alone.
> You must love the Lord your God with all your heart and with all your soul and with all your might.
> Take to heart these words with which I charge you this day. (Deuteronomy 6:4-6.)

> If, then, you obey the commandments that I enjoin upon you this day, loving the Lord your God and serving Him with all your heart and soul,
> I will grant the rain for your land in season . . . .
> Therefore impress these my words upon your very heart. (Deuteronomy 11:13-14, 18.)

> The Lord spoke to Moses, saying:
> Speak to the Israelite people and instruct them to . . . recall all the commandments of the Lord and observe them, so that you do not follow your heart and eyes in your lustful urge. (Numbers 15:37-39.)

After giving Israel the Ten Commandments, the Lord said to Moses:

> O that there were such an heart in them, that they would fear me, and keep all my commandments always, that it might be well with them, and with their children for ever! (Deuteronomy 5:29).

Unfortunately, the children of Israel were "a stiff-necked people, quick to do iniquity, and slow to remember the Lord their God." Therefore, the Lord gave them "a law of performances and of ordinances, a law which they were to observe strictly from day to day, to keep them in remembrance of God and their duty towards him." (Mosiah 13:29–30.) Nevertheless, the more exacting commandments pertaining to thoughts remained in force. Thus the prophet Isaiah commanded: "Let the wicked forsake his way, and the unrighteous man his thoughts" (Isaiah 55:7).

During the Savior's earthly mission, he gave commandments that reemphasized motives, desires, and attitudes.

Motives

Jesus looked beyond the actions of the scribes and Pharisees and condemned them because of their motives. He likened them to "whited sepulchres," which appear beautiful outside but are unclean inside. Although their actions he referred to were appropriate, they were acting for the wrong reasons. "Even so ye also outwardly appear righteous unto men," he told them, "but within ye are full of hypocrisy and iniquity" (Matthew 23:27-28). In contrast, in choosing his disciples Jesus praised Nathanael as "an Israelite indeed, in whom is no guile" (John 1:47).

Desires

The Savior also taught the importance of our desires. "Blessed are they which do hunger and thirst after righteousness," he taught in the Sermon on the Mount (Matthew 5:6; 3 Nephi 12:6). The scriptures say that when we desire righteousness our "heart is right" with God. The Psalmist condemned the people of ancient Israel because "their heart was not right with [God]" (Psalm 78:37). When King Solomon blessed the people at the dedication of the temple, he concluded with these words: "Let your heart therefore be perfect with the Lord our God, to walk in his statutes, and to keep his commandments, as at this day" (1 Kings 8:61).

Our priorities determine what we seek in life. As we read in modern revelation: "Seek not for riches but for wisdom, and behold, the mysteries of God shall be unfolded unto you, and then shall you be made rich. Behold, he that hath eternal life is rich."

In a letter written to W. W. Phelps in 1833, the Prophet Joseph Smith used these same phrases:

> Remember God sees the secret springs of human action, & knows the hearts of all living. . . . It is also useless to make[e] great pretentions when the heart is not right before God, for God looks at the heart. (D. Jessee, *The Personal Writings of Joseph Smith* [Salt Lake City: Deseret Book Co., 1984], pp. 263-64.)

Our heart is right or perfect with God when we desire what God desires.

Attitudes and Priorities

If our heart is right, we also have righteous attitudes and priorities.

Our attitudes determine how we react to life's experiences. For example, Jesus taught us how to react to persecution:

> Blessed are ye, when men shall revile you, and persecute you, and shall say all manner of evil against you falsely, for my sake.
>
> Rejoice, and be exceeding glad: for great is your reward in heaven: for so persecuted they the prophets which were before you. (Matthew 5:11-12.)

Our priorities determine what we seek in life. "Wherefore, seek not the things of this world but seek ye first to build up the kingdom of God, and to establish his righteousness" (*JST* Matthew 6:38), Jesus taught his disciples. As we read in modern revelation: "Seek not for riches but for wisdom, and behold, the mysteries of God shall be unfolded unto you, and then shall you be made rich. Behold, he that hath eternal life is rich." (D&C 6:7.)

The qualities we call materialism and spirituality are expressive of priorities and attitudes toward the nature and purpose of life.

Thoughts

Jesus also commanded his followers to purify their thoughts. Our behavior is shaped by the nature of our thoughts. In this way we are the product of our thoughts. We are all familiar with the proverb, "For as he thinketh in his heart, so is he" (Proverbs 23:7). This is why the Apostle Paul counseled the Philippians to "think on" things that were honest, pure, and lovely (Philippians 4:8).

The divine concern with our thoughts has been echoed and explained in modern revelation and in the words of modern prophets. "Look unto me in every thought" (D&C 6:36), the Lord instructed the young prophet, Joseph Smith. President David O. McKay declared: "The thought in your mind at this moment is contributing, however infinitesimally, almost imperceptibly to the shaping of your soul" (quoted in Spencer W. Kimball, *The Miracle of Forgiveness* [Salt Lake City: Bookcraft, 1969], p. 105).

In his book *The Miracle of Forgiveness* (pages 108 and 103), Elder Spencer W. Kimball elaborated on this principle in a chapter titled "As a Man Thinketh." He referred to "our thought sins," which "are recorded in heaven." As to this, he taught: "A man is literally what he thinks, his character being the complete sum of all his thoughts."

Elder David B. Haight gave us an example of this principle in his description of how pornography affects a person's thoughts and then his behavior:

> Continued exposure desensitizes the spirit and can erode the conscience of unwary people. A victim becomes a slave to carnal thoughts and actions. As the thought is father to the deed, exposure can lead to acting out what is nurtured in the mind. ("Personal Morality," *Ensign*, November 1984, p. 70.)

President Ezra Taft Benson related this principle to our free agency:

> You are the one who must decide whose thoughts you will entertain. You are free to choose—but you are not free to alter the consequences of those choices. You will be what you think about—what you consistently allow to occupy the stage of your mind. (Ezra Taft Benson, "Think on Christ," *Ensign*, April 1984, p. 11.)

Judging the Inner Man

The scriptures teach that in the final judgment we will be held responsible for our thoughts. This principle of accountability, whose scriptural basis is discussed hereafter, highlights a critical contrast between the laws of God and the laws of man.

The laws of man, with which I was preoccupied in my thirty years in the legal profession, are not concerned with a person's motives or desires in isolation. When the law inquires into a person's intent or state of mind, it only seeks to determine what consequence should be assigned to particular actions that person has taken.

In contrast, the laws of God are concerned with spiritual things. Spiritual things are affected by motives, desires,

> **The laws of God are concerned with spiritual things. Spiritual things are affected by motives, desires, and attitudes independent of actions. Gospel consequences flow from our thoughts.**

and attitudes independent of actions. Gospel consequences flow from our thoughts.

A simple example illustrates that contrast. Suppose a homeowner has a beautiful car parked in his driveway. His neighbor is attracted to it, but takes no action. He just looks on it longingly, and covets it. He has sinned. He has broken one of the laws of God (Exodus 20:17). Eternal consequences follow.

Up to this point the neighbor has not broken any of the laws of man. However, if he takes a particular action, such as crossing the ignition wires and driving away in the car, he has committed a wrong that can be punished under the law.

To determine what legal consequence should be assigned to the neighbor's action, we would inquire into his intent in taking the car. If he simply intended to borrow the car in the mistaken belief that the owner would consent, he might not be guilty of a crime. (However, he would be liable for damages for the wrongful use of the car.) If he intended to use the car contrary to the wishes of the owner and yet return it in a short time, he would have committed a minor crime. If he intended to take the car permanently, he would have committed a major crime. To choose among these various alternatives, a judge or jury would attempt to determine his intent ("state of mind") at the time he took the car.

As a second example, suppose a person signs a document, such as a will or a contract, and later contends that it was invalid because he signed it under duress or in jest. The law makes provision for a judge or jury to try to determine the state of mind with which the document was signed: Did the person who signed it intend that his signature make it a valid will or contract? If he did not, the document has no legal effect.

These examples illustrate how the laws of man sometimes inquire into a person's state of mind in order to determine the consequences of particular actions. But the law will never punish or give effect to motives, desires, or attitudes standing alone.

It is good that this is so. The law is an imperfect instrument. It has no reliable way to look into a person's mind or heart. It must judge intent on the basis of what can be experienced through the five senses: overt actions in the context of observed circumstances.

So it was in Book of Mormon times. As we read in Alma, the people of Nephi were punished for their criminal actions, but "there was no law against a man's belief" (Alma 30:7, 11). Alma gives the reason for this distinction: "It was strictly contrary to the commands of God that there should be a law which should bring men on to unequal grounds" (Alma 30:7). In other words, men were free to choose: to believe in God and desire to serve him, or not to believe in God and not desire to serve him (Alma 30:8-9). Their right to choose—their free agency—was safeguarded by prohibiting laws that would penalize a person's making one mental choice or the other, since this would "bring men on to unequal grounds" (Alma 30:7). The civil laws of that day only punished criminal *actions*; "Therefore all men were on equal grounds" (Alma 30:10-11).

In contrast, God's law can assign consequences solely on the basis of our innermost thoughts. There is no failure of proof in the ultimate administration of God's law. As we read in Proverbs: "All the ways of a man are clean in his own eyes; but the Lord weigheth the spirits" (Proverbs 16:2).

When the prophet Samuel was sent to Bethlehem to choose and anoint one of the sons of Jesse as a new king for Israel, the Lord told him to reject the first son, though he was a man of fine appearance. The Lord explained: "Look not on his countenance, or on the height of his stature; because I have refused him: for the Lord seeth not as man seeth; for man looketh on outward appearance, but the Lord looketh on the heart" (1 Samuel 16:7).

The Savior told the Pharisees, "God knoweth your hearts" (Luke 16:15). Paul warned the Hebrews that God "is a discerner of the thoughts and intents of the heart," and that "all things are naked and opened unto the eyes of him with whom we have to do" (Hebrews 4:12-13; see also 1 Corinthians 4:5). Ammon taught his people that God "knows all the thoughts and intents of the heart; for by his hand were they all created from the beginning" (Alma 18:32; also see Mosiah 24:12; D&C 6:16). And Mormon wrote, "for none is acceptable before God, save the meek and lowly in heart" (Moroni 7:44).

In this dispensation, the Lord has reaffirmed that God "is a discerner of the thoughts and intents of the heart" (D&C 33:1). Elder John Taylor said:

> He knows our thoughts and comprehends our desires and feelings; he knows our acts and the motives which prompt us to perform them. He is acquainted with all the doings and operations of the human family, and all the secret thoughts and acts of the children of men are open and naked before him, and for them he will bring them to judgment. (*Journal of Discourses* 16:301-2.)

In other words, God knows who is pure in heart. He can and will judge us not only for our actions but also for our

10

We have free agency. We exercise that free agency not only by what we do but also by what we decide—what we choose to will or desire. Restrictions on freedom can deprive us of the power or freedom to act, but no one can deprive us of the power to will or desire. Free agency is an eternal principle. So is accountability for its exercise. Accountability must reach and attach consequences to our motives, desires, and attitudes.

---

motives, desires, and attitudes. This reality is challenging, but not surprising.

We have free agency. We exercise that free agency not only by what we *do* but also by what we *decide*—what we choose to will or desire. Restrictions on freedom can deprive us of the power or freedom *to act*, but no one can deprive us of the power to *will* or *desire*. Free agency is an eternal principle. So is accountability for its exercise. Accountability must reach and attach consequences to our motives, desires, and attitudes.

This accountability will punish us for sinful thoughts and reward us for righteous ones. As we learn in modern scripture, during the events connected with the Second Coming, God will "reveal the secret acts of men, and the thoughts and intents of their hearts" (D&C 88:109).

Brigham Young taught: "We shall be judged according to the deeds done in the body and according to the thoughts and intents of the heart" (John A. Widtsoe, ed., *Discourses of Brigham Young* [Salt Lake City: Deseret Book Co., 1941], p. 382).

Karl G. Maeser, the great leader of Brigham Young Academy, told his students: "Not only will you be held accountable for the things you do, but you will be held responsible for the very thoughts you think." For a time that teaching troubled his young student George Albert Smith. Then he understood. As he said later:

> Why, of course you will be held accountable for your thoughts, because when your life is completed in mortality, it will be the sum of your thoughts. That one suggestion has been a great blessing to me all my life, and it has enabled me upon many occasions to avoid thinking improperly, because I realize that I will be, when my life's labor is complete, the product of my thoughts. (George Albert Smith, *Sharing the Gospel with Others* [Salt Lake City: Deseret Book Co., 1948], pp. 62–63, quoted by Ezra Taft Benson in "Think on Christ," *Ensign*, April 1984, p. 10.)

This accountability is clearly taught in the scriptures. In modern revelation the Lord has declared: "I, the Lord, will judge all men according to their works, according to the desire of their hearts" (D&C 137:9). Alma declared:

> [God] granteth unto men according to their desire, whether it be unto death or unto life; . . . according to their wills, whether they be unto salvation or unto destruction. Yea, . . . he that knoweth good and evil, to him it is given according to his desires (Alma 29:4–5; see also D&C 7:8; 11:8).

The capacity to reward for righteous motives, desires, and attitudes illustrates another contrast between the laws of God and the laws of man. It is entirely impractical to grant a *legal* advantage on the basis of an intent or desire not translated into action. "I intended to sign that contract" or "We intended to get married" cannot substitute for the act required by law. If the laws of man gave effect to intentions or desires in place of required acts, it would open the door for too much abuse, since these laws and those who enforce them have no reliable means of determining our innermost thoughts or desires.

In contrast, the laws of God can reward a righteous desire or attitude because an omniscient God can determine it. If a person does not perform a particular commandment because he is genuinely unable to do so, but truly would if he could, our Heavenly Father will know this and will reward that person accordingly.

Upon the same principle, evil thoughts or desires are sinful under the laws of God even though not translated into the actions that would make them punishable under the laws of man. Similarly, if a person performs a seemingly righteous act but does so for the wrong reasons, such as to achieve a selfish purpose, his *hands* may be clean but his *heart* is not "pure." His act will not be counted for righteousness.

Subsequent chapters will discuss and provide the scriptural authority for these assertions. The motives or states of mind with which we act are explored in chapters 2 and 3. The effects of desires that are not accompanied by actions are discussed in chapter 4. The succeeding three chapters examine different mental attitudes or priorities by which we evaluate our life's experiences: materialism, pride, and spirituality. Chapter 8 describes the condition of mind that constitutes the attitude of worship. Chapter 9 suggests things we can do to become pure in heart.

CHAPTER TWO

MOTIVE AND REAL INTENT

We must not only *do* what is right. We must act for the right reasons. The modern term is *good motive*. The scriptures often signify this appropriate mental attitude with the words *full purpose of heart* or *real intent*.

The scriptures make clear that God understands our motives and will judge our actions accordingly. If we do not act for the right reasons, our acts will not be counted for righteousness.

The Apostle Paul teaches this principle in his famous statement about the "letter" and the "spirit." He introduces the thought by discussing his own motives in the ministry. He explains that he needed no epistle of commendation because the Saints of Corinth were the certification of his ministry for Christ. That certification was "written not with ink, but with the Spirit of the living God; not in tables of stone, but in fleshy tables of the heart." Paul's "sufficiency" was not in himself, he says, or in any external evidences (like tables of stone), but "of God," who had made him a minister "of the new testament." (2 Corinthians 3:1, 3, 5, 6.)

Paul's next words describe the nature and intent of his ministry: "Not of the letter, but of the spirit: for the letter killeth, but the spirit giveth life" (2 Corinthians 3:6). Just as it is the spirit that identifies and gives life to the ministry, so it is the motive that gives life and legitimacy to the acts of the believer.

Priestcraft

The Book of Mormon applies this principle to those who seem to be serving the Lord but do so with a hidden motive to gain personal advantage rather than to further the work of the Lord: "Priestcrafts are that men preach and set themselves up for a light unto the world, that they may get gain and praise of the world; but they seek not the welfare of Zion" (2 Nephi 26:29; see also Alma 1:16).

Priestcraft is the sin committed by the combination of a good act—such as preaching or teaching the gospel—and a bad motive. The act may be good and visible, but the sin is in the motive. On earth, the wrong motive may be known only to the actor, but in heaven it is always known to God.

An early experience of the Prophet Joseph Smith's provides an illustration of the importance of proper motive in the service of the Lord. When the young prophet first went to Cumorah, in 1823, the angel refused to give him the plates containing the Book of Mormon, saying it was not yet time (Joseph Smith–History 1:53). During the four years he had to wait before receiving the plates, young Joseph struggled with his motives. In 1832 he looked back on this period and wrote:

I had been tempted of the advisary and saught the Plates to obtain riches and kept not the commandment that I should

It is easier to have clean hands than to have a pure heart. It is easier to control our acts than to control our thoughts. The requirement that our good acts must be accompanied by good motives is subtle and difficult in practice.

---

have an eye single to the glory of God therefore I was chastened and saught diligently to obtain the plates and obtained them not until I was twenty one years of age (D. Jessee, *The Personal Writings of Joseph Smith*, p. 7).

In this revealing account we find the Lord seeing into the heart of the young prophet, chastening him for his improper motives in respect to the plates, giving him time to repent and mature, and eventually forgiving him and allowing him to go forward with the performance of his mission.

The sin of priestcraft is a grievous one. Time after time the Lord has condemned those who appear to men to be his servants, but who, though they draw near to him with their lips, have removed their hearts far from him. This description of those who have no true motive to serve the Lord appears in Isaiah (29:13), in Matthew (15:8), in 2 Nephi (27:25), and in Joseph Smith's History (JS–H 1:19). In modern as in ancient times, those who appear to be servants of the Lord and present themselves to labor in his vineyard are subject to the prophetic principle: "The laborer in Zion shall labor for Zion; for if they labor for money they shall perish" (2 Nephi 26:31).

The prototype of those who appear to serve God but actually have other motives is King Amaziah, who "did that which was right in the sight of the Lord, but not with a perfect heart" (2 Chronicles 25:2).

During my lifetime, I have seen more than a few persons in positions of responsibility in various churches whose activities in the "work of the Lord" seemed to be motivated predominantly by personal interest. The commandment to avoid priestcraft is a vital challenge to religious persons in every age of time.

The Requirement of a Good Motive

It is easier to have clean hands than to have a pure heart. It is easier to control our acts than to control our thoughts. The requirement that our good acts must be accompanied by good motives is subtle and difficult in practice.

The first temptation offered to the Savior was of this character. To "an hungred" Jesus, the tempter said, "If thou be the Son of God, command that these stones be made bread" (Matthew 4:2-3). "Why not?" Elder McConkie asks (*The Mortal Messiah* [Salt Lake City: Deseret Book Co., 1979], 1:411). There was nothing wrong with the Lord's providing food by miraculous means. He had provided the children of Israel with manna in the wilderness. He would soon turn water into wine in Cana, and he would later multiply loaves and fishes so that thousands could eat.

The proposed *act* was appropriate, but in this circumstance the *motive* would have been wrong. As Elder McConkie explains, Lucifer challenged Jesus to perform a miracle for the purpose of proving his divinity, a fact that needed no proof (see *The Mortal Messiah*, 1:412). The performance of a miracle for that purpose would have been inappropriate, like the giving of a sign. Jesus declined the temptation, answering, "It is written, Man shall not live by bread alone, but by every word that proceedeth out of the mouth of God" (Matthew 4:4).

The principle that we must act for the right reasons has many illustrations in the scriptures.

Seeking a Testimony of the Book of Mormon

One of the most significant expressions of the importance of motive occurs in the promise of Moroni. He uses the term "real intent":

> And when ye shall receive these things, I would exhort you that ye would ask God, the Eternal Father, in the name of Christ, if these things are not true; and if ye shall ask with a sincere heart, *with real intent*, having faith in Christ, he will manifest the truth of it unto you, by the power of the Holy Ghost (Moroni 10:4; italics added).

Like most Latter-day Saints, I have had the experience of sharing a copy of the Book of Mormon with a sincere Christian friend who later claimed to have read it and prayed about it and received no witness. How can this be? Is the promise of the prophet Moroni subject to exceptions?

There are doubtless instances in which individuals do not obtain a witness because they have not "received" (read and pondered [Moroni 10:3]) the book, or in which, even though they have read and pondered it, they have not prayed "with a sincere heart."

The meaning of the words *with real intent* also explains why some prayerful and sincere seekers receive no witness. To qualify for the promise of Moroni, a prayer about the truthfulness of the Book of Mormon must be made for the right reason. "With real intent" means that if the Holy Ghost witnesses the truth of the book, the prayerful seeker is committed to act on that witness by being baptized into The Church of Jesus Christ of Latter-day Saints.

Moroni did not promise a manifestation of the Holy Ghost to those who seek to know the truth of the Book of

Moroni did not promise a manifestation of the Holy Ghost to those who seek to know the truth of the Book of Mormon for hypothetical or academic reasons, even if they "ask with a sincere heart." The promise of Moroni is for those who are committed in their hearts to act upon the manifestation if it is received. Prayers based on any other reason have no promise because they are not made "with real intent."

Mormon for hypothetical or academic reasons, even if they "ask with a sincere heart." The promise of Moroni is for those who are committed in their hearts to act upon the manifestation if it is received. Prayers based on any other reason have no promise because they are not made "with real intent."

The Holy Ghost does not answer hypothetical or academic questions, for that would be to give a sign. As we know, "Faith cometh not by signs, but signs follow those that believe" (D&C 63:9). The Lord has revealed that spiritual gifts are given "that all may be benefited that seek or that ask of me, that ask and not for a sign" (D&C 46:9). When sincere truth-seekers exercise their faith in God by praying "with a sincere heart, with real intent," they are not asking for a sign, and the manifestation of the truth of the Book of Mormon will follow.

Conversion

The Book of Mormon teaches that our conversion—our coming unto Christ—must be done with full purpose of heart. The prophet Nephi declared:

> Wherefore, my beloved brethren, I know that if ye shall follow the Son, with full purpose of heart, acting no

hypocrisy and no deception before God, but with real intent, repenting of your sins, witnessing unto the Father that ye are willing to take upon you the name of Christ, by baptism— yea, by following your Lord and your Savior down into the water, according to his word, behold, then shall ye receive the Holy Ghost (2 Nephi 31:13).

The converted King Limhi promised his people that the Lord would deliver them from bondage if they would "turn to the Lord with full purpose of heart" (Mosiah 7:33).

During his ministry among the Nephites, the Savior said, "Come unto me with full purpose of heart, and I will receive you" (3 Nephi 12:24; see also Mormon 9:27).

Repentance and Baptism

Repentance must also be accomplished "with full purpose of heart." Among the first words the Savior uttered when he appeared to the people on the American continent were these: "O ye house of Israel whom I have spared, how oft will I gather you as a hen gathereth her chickens under her wings, if ye will repent and return unto me with full purpose of heart" (3 Nephi 10:6).

The Savior later commanded the Nephites to "repent of your sins, and come unto me with a broken heart and a contrite spirit" (3 Nephi 12:19). A later prophet recorded of his people that "as oft as they repented and sought forgiveness, with real intent, they were forgiven" (Moroni 6:8). In our own day the Lord has commanded us to forgive one who "has committed adultery and repents with all his heart, and forsaketh it, and doeth it no more" (D&C 42:25).

What do these scriptures have to say about the person whose conversion, repentance, or baptism into the Church is motivated by something other than "full purpose of

21

heart'' or ''a broken heart and a contrite spirit''? What of the person who is swept into the gospel net by the currents of social pressure? What of the person whose motive for seeking Church membership is economic advantage? What of the person who seeks or maintains fellowship in the Church out of business necessity or political expediency? The Lord answered such questions in a revelation given to the convert, W. W. Phelps: ''Behold, . . . thou art called and chosen; and after thou hast been baptized by water, which if you do with an eye single to my glory, you shall have a remission of your sins and a reception of the Holy Spirit by the laying on of hands'' (D&C 55:1).

In his great prophecy of the future Messiah, Father Lehi taught his son Jacob:

> Wherefore, redemption cometh in and through the Holy Messiah; for he is full of grace and truth.
>
> Behold, he offereth himself a sacrifice for sin, to answer the ends of the law, unto all those who have a broken heart and a contrite spirit; and unto none else can the ends of the law be answered. (2 Nephi 2:6–7; see also D&C 21:9.)

Similarly, the risen Lord told the Nephites: ''And whoso cometh unto me with a broken heart and a contrite spirit, him will I baptize with fire and with the Holy Ghost'' (3 Nephi 9:20). The blessings of remission of sins and reception of the Holy Ghost are stated to be contingent upon the attitude of our hearts.

Giving to the Poor

In his teachings to the people of both the Old World and the New, the Savior stressed that those who give to the poor ''to be seen of men'' have acted to obtain an earthly reward and will receive no reward in heaven:

Clearly, unless motivated by pure love, even the most generous gifts of earthly treasures "profiteth . . . nothing."

> Verily, verily, I say that I would that ye should do alms unto the poor; but take heed that ye do not your alms before men to be seen of them; otherwise ye have no reward of your Father who is in heaven.
>
> Therefore, when ye shall do your alms do not sound a trumpet before you, as will hypocrites do in the synagogues and in the streets, that they may have glory of men. Verily I say unto you, they have their reward. (3 Nephi 13:1-2; see also Matthew 6:1-3.)

This may be the clearest of all scriptural teachings on the importance of doing the right things for the right reasons.

The Apostle Paul echoed this fundamental truth of Christianity in his great sermon on charity: "And though I bestow all my goods to feed the poor, and though I give my body to be burned, and have not charity, it profiteth me nothing" (1 Corinthians 13:3). Clearly, unless motivated by pure love, even the most generous gifts of earthly treasures "profiteth . . . nothing." As Paul would later counsel Timothy: "Now the end of the commandment is charity out of a pure heart, and of a good conscience, and of faith unfeigned" (1 Timothy 1:5).

Prayer and Fasting

Prayer and fasting are other activities that must be undertaken for the right reasons. Those who do these sacred acts in order to be seen of men have their reward on earth and not in heaven. Jesus taught:

> And when thou prayest thou shalt not do as the hypocrites, for they love to pray, standing in the synagogues and in the corners of the streets, that they may be seen of men. Verily I say unto you, they have their reward.
>
> But when ye pray, use not vain repetitions, as the heathen, for they think that they shall be heard for their much speaking. (3 Nephi 13:5, 7; also Matthew 6:5, 7).

The Book of Mormon prophets affirmed this teaching both before and after the appearance of the risen Christ. Alma pleaded with one of his sons not to pray as the Zoramites, "to be heard of men, and to be praised for their wisdom" (Alma 38:13). Mormon observed that "the Lord is merciful unto all who will, in the sincerity of their hearts, call upon his holy name" (Helaman 3:27).

Mormon was most emphatic that prayers offered without "real intent of heart" would evoke no blessings: "And likewise also is it counted evil unto a man, if he shall pray and not with real intent of heart; yea, and it profiteth him nothing, for God receiveth none such" (Moroni 7:9).

It is significant that the prayer that was answered with the First Vision was heartfelt. Joseph Smith recalled, "I kneeled down and began to offer up the desires of my heart to God" (Joseph Smith–History 1:15). Prayers come before the throne of grace when they are made with faith and when they represent the true desires of the heart. In modern revelation the Lord instructed those assembled at a particular conference, describing them as elders "whose prayers I have heard, and whose hearts I know, and whose desires have come up before me" (D&C 67:1).

To be spiritually effective, fasting must also be done with a sincere, righteous purpose, not for the selfish reason of being seen and admired of men.

> Moreover, when ye fast be not as the hypocrites, of a sad countenance, for they disfigure their faces that they may

appear unto men to fast. Verily I say unto you, they have their reward.

But thou, when thou fastest, anoint thy head, and wash thy face;

That thou appear not unto men to fast, but unto thy Father, who is in secret; and thy Father, who seeth in secret, shall reward thee openly. (3 Nephi 13:16-18; also Matthew: 6:16-18.)

The Savior's commandments on the mental attitudes that should accompany prayer and fasting, like the Beatitudes and other teachings of this supreme sermon, establish an exquisitely difficult standard for mortals. As F. W. Farrar observed in his great work *The Life of Christ* (London: Cassell & Co., Ltd., 1874):

It is easy to be a slave to the letter, and difficult to enter into the spirit; easy to obey a number of outward rules, difficult to enter intelligently and self-sacrificingly into the will of God; easy to entangle the soul in a network of petty observances, difficult to yield the obedience of an enlightened heart; easy to be haughtily exclusive, difficult to be humbly spiritual; easy to be an ascetic or a formalist, difficult to be pure, and loving, and wise, and free; easy to be a Pharisee, difficult to be a disciple; very easy to embrace a self-satisfying and sanctimonious system of rabbinical observances, very difficult to love God with all the heart, and all the might, and all the soul, and all the strength. (Page 469, quoted in Bruce R. McConkie, *The Mortal Messiah* [Salt Lake City: Deseret Book Co., 1980], 3:232.)

Seeking and Questioning

Motive is also important in our quest for knowledge and in the questioning that accompanies it. In commenting on our duty to educate for eternity, Eugene England writes:

Teaching—or learning—with the Spirit of God simply means (though it is not simple) that we are doing so with an eye single to eternal, not worldly, values, with an eye single to lasting development of the mind and spirit and to useful service to others, especially to aid in *their* lasting development of mind and spirit. (*Why the Church Is as True as the Gospel* [Salt Lake City: Bookcraft, 1986], p. 86.)

Seeking and questioning can be a pathway to learning and service, or it can be a means of disruption and self-aggrandizement. The questions can be the same in both instances. The difference is in the questioners' motives. One person can be seeking knowledge "with an eye single to eternal . . . values," while another person asking the same questions can be seeking nothing more than to sow discontent and to reap profit or prominence. During more than a quarter of a century of active participation in intellectual pursuits, as a student, teacher, and administrator in universities, I have seen Latter-day Saint seeking and questioning of both types. I continue to see this contrast in the letters and articles I read as a General Authority of the Church. Participants in both types of seeking and questioning could frame their questions more precisely and evaluate responses more wisely if they were more aware of the nature and importance of their personal motives. Sadly, suggestions to read the scriptures for guidance sometimes go unheeded, and more direct counsel is sometimes resented as coercive.

Sabbath Observance

A Sabbath law that codifies certain acts as forbidden is pharisaical. Here, as much as in any area of gospel observance, "the letter killeth, but the spirit giveth life" (2 Corinthians 3:6).

In terms of the appropriateness of various Sabbath activities, our actions are sometimes less important than

In terms of the appropriateness of various Sabbath activities, our actions are sometimes less important than our motives. An action that is wrong with one motive may be right with another. We look to the purpose of the Sabbath to identify the motives by which our Sabbath activities should be regulated.

---

our motives. An action that is wrong with one motive may be right with another. It is the motive that determines whether a Sabbath excursion is a joyride or an errand of compassion.

We look to the purpose of the Sabbath to identify the motives by which our Sabbath activities should be regulated.

The Sabbath was blessed and sanctified as a holy day, a day of rest (Genesis 2:3; Moses 3:3; Exodus 20:9–11). But this sanctification and commandment of rest was for a purpose—not that man should refrain from work in order to pursue his own pleasure, but that man should serve God and worship him. The prophet Isaiah taught that principle clearly:

> If thou turn away thy foot from the sabbath, from doing thy pleasure on my holy day; and call the sabbath a delight, the holy of the Lord, honourable; and shalt honour him, not doing thine own ways, nor finding thine own pleasure, nor speaking thine own words:
>
> Then shalt thou delight thyself in the Lord; and I will cause thee to ride upon the high places of the earth, and feed thee with the heritage of Jacob thy father: for the mouth of the Lord hath spoken it. (Isaiah 58:13–14.)

When the Pharisees challenged his disciples for the acts of plucking and eating grain on the Sabbath, Jesus denounced their formalism, which forbade acts regardless of intent. He reaffirmed the true law of the Sabbath:

27

> And he said unto them, The Sabbath was made for man, and not man for the Sabbath.
>
> Wherefore the Sabbath was given unto man for a day of rest; and also that man should glorify God, and not that man should not eat. (JST Mark 2:25–26.)

The same principles are reaffirmed in modern revelation, where the Sabbath is described as a holy day whose purpose is "that thou mayest . . . keep thyself unspotted from the world" (D&C 59:9).

What activities are commanded on the Sabbath? The revelation states:

> Thou shalt go to the house of prayer and offer up thy sacraments upon my holy day;
>
> For verily this is a day appointed unto you to rest from your labors, and to pay thy devotions unto the Most High. (D&C 59:9–10.)

Succeeding verses warn the Sabbath observer against activities that are contrary to this spirit:

> And on this day thou shalt do none other thing, only let thy food be prepared with singleness of heart that thy fasting may be perfect, or, in other words, that thy joy may be full.
>
> Verily, this is fasting and prayer, or in other words, rejoicing and prayer. (D&C 59:13–14.)

Then there is a promise, similar to the prophet Isaiah's:

> And inasmuch as ye do these things with thanksgiving, with cheerful hearts and countenances, not with much laughter, for this is sin, but with a glad heart and a cheerful countenance—
>
> Verily I say, that inasmuch as ye do this, the fulness of the earth is yours, the beasts of the field and the fowls of the air, and that which climbeth upon the trees and walketh upon the earth. (D&C 59:15–16.)

President Spencer W. Kimball put our teaching on Sabbath observance in a nutshell when he suggested that we "measure each Sabbath activity by the yardstick of worshipfulness" (*The Teachings of Spencer W. Kimball*, Edward L. Kimball, ed. [Salt Lake City: Bookcraft, 1982], p. 219).

The nature of worship and its dependence on the worshipper's attitude of spirit and mind are discussed in chapter 8.

Service to God

A person earns no blessings for acts of service that are coerced or are performed with feelings of resentment. The Lord warned the children of Israel that they should serve him "with joyfulness, and with gladness of heart" (Deuteronomy 28:47). In the present dispensation, the Lord has promised choice blessings to those who keep his commandments "with thanksgiving, with cheerful hearts and countenances" (D&C 59:15). That promise is even extended to those who serve and worship through song: "For my soul delighteth in the song of the heart; yea, the song of the righteous is a prayer unto me, and it shall be answered with a blessing upon their heads" (D&C 25:12).

The Lord praised the prophet Nephi, the son of Helaman, because he had "with unwearyingness declared the word." The Lord also praised him because "thou hast not feared [this people], and hast not sought thine own life, but hast sought my will, and to keep my commandments" (Helaman 10:4). Here was a prophet who had not only done what the Lord commanded him but had done it in complete and unselfish fulfillment of the will of the Lord. The Lord rewarded him with this promise:

> And now, because thou hast done this with such unwearyingness, behold, I will bless thee forever; and I will make thee mighty in word and in deed, in faith and in works; yea, even that all things shall be done unto thee according to

thy word, for thou shalt not ask that which is contrary to my will (Helaman 10:5).

Such is an example to all of us.

In contrast, the risen Lord warned his people to "beware of false prophets, who come to you in sheep's clothing, but inwardly they are ravening wolves" (3 Nephi 14:15). In every age there are those whose outward appearance and actions seem appropriate but whose inward motives make them as dangerous to the flock of God as "ravening wolves." Such a one is the person who pretends to a desire to *help* others but really only desires to *use* others. In the world of business, this includes the scheming promoter whose pretense of helping a customer masks the reality that he is only using the customer to achieve his own selfish purposes.

The contrast between the motive to help and the motive to use can even be seen in some Church service. A missionary with a motive to use "his" mission for personal growth and "his" baptisms to gain recognition for "his" accomplishments is a phony and a failure. His motives and attitudes are transparent. Companions, leaders, and investigators will soon recognize and resent a missionary who sees them as mere objects to be used for his benefit.

A missionary who sees himself (or herself) as a servant of the Lord, an instrument in his hands to do his work (Alma 17:9), has the motive to *help* others. That attitude and motive is transparent also, and its fruits are trust and love from all with whom the missionary associates.

This same principle applies to presidents and bishops, to teachers and temple workers. All must seek to serve as instruments of God's purposes rather than as promoters of their own. As Jesus taught:

> If any man will come after me, let him deny himself, and take up his cross, and follow me.

For whosoever will save his life shall lose it: and whosoever will lose his life for my sake shall find it. (Matthew 16:24–25.)

The various motives for service are discussed further in the next chapter.

The Active and the Less Active

Motive or attitude is also an important consideration in the status we refer to as Church "activity." In the Church we tend to think of members in categories according to "activity": active, less active, inactive, and so on. These categories are defined according to observable actions, notably attendance at Church meetings. They take little or no account (positive or negative) of the things of the heart. This is a misleading omission.

A person may love God with all his or her heart, might, mind, and strength, and still be in a circumstance in which it is impossible or extremely difficult to do the actions that are customarily judged to constitute "activity." What category should we assign to the man whom I heard say to a Church audience, "I was inactive to the extent of not attending meetings, but never inactive to the extent of not loving the Lord"? That attitude can be a self-serving rationalization, or it can be a sincere manifestation of an intent to comply with the direction to show our love of the Lord by keeping his commandments.

Even where a person is "less active" because of carelessness or indifference, it is well to remember that the contrast between this member and some apparently active members may be quite different than meets the eye. Consider the contrast between deficiencies in actions and deficiencies in motives and attitudes. Who is more acceptable to God, a man who is indifferent to God and his fellowmen but attends church regularly to promote his

We should all realize, as Stephen R. Covey has
observed, that "going through motions or
perfunctorily fulfilling one's calling in order to meet
minimum expectations is insufficient in doing the
work of the Lord and blessing the lives of others." All
of us should seek the kind of activity that "has to do
with the heart and mind of man as well as the location
of his body."

---

business interests, or a man who loves God and his fellowmen but rarely attends meetings? Both of these men are
missing blessings and growth. Both have need to change.
But which is in a better position to bring himself into total
harmony with God? Attendance patterns can be altered in
an instant. A new resolve, proven by subsequent conduct,
can repair inaction. But a defect of the heart is much more
serious and requires far more time and effort to repair.

We should all realize, as Stephen R. Covey has observed, that "going through motions or perfunctorily fulfilling one's calling in order to meet minimum expectations
is insufficient in doing the work of the Lord and blessing
the lives of others." All of us should seek the kind of activity that "has to do with the heart and mind of man as well
as the location of his body." (*The Divine Center* [Salt Lake
City: Bookcraft, 1982], pp. 52–53.)

The so-called "less active" man who still loves the Lord
and his fellowmen and is loyal to the Church and its
mission can be closer to full acceptability to the Lord than
the man whose "activity" is exemplary but whose motives
are personal rather than Christian. This is why we make
such an effort to welcome back the less active and why
many of them can quickly turn into some of our most faithful members and most effective leaders.

Without Proper Motive It Profiteth Nothing

Up to this point we have considered a variety of acts that we would call good, such as conversion, repentance, baptism, giving to the poor, and service to God and fellow-man. The scriptures teach that to obtain blessings by these good acts we must do them with the right motive.

With unequalled clarity and emphatic repetition, the prophet Mormon taught the people of his day:

> For behold, God hath said a man being evil cannot do that which is good; for if he offereth a gift, . . . except he shall do it with real intent it profiteth him nothing.
>
> For behold, it is not counted unto him for righteousness. (Moroni 7:6–7.)

The consequences of an improper motive: the giver's gift "profiteth him nothing" and "is not counted unto him for righteousness." As if the point were not clear enough already, Mormon adds:

> For behold, if a man being evil giveth a gift, he doeth it grudgingly; wherefore it is counted unto him the same as if he had retained the gift; wherefore he is counted evil before God (Moroni 7:8).

President David O. McKay taught:

> Mere compliance with the word of the Lord, without a corresponding inward desire, will avail but little. Indeed, such outward actions and pretending phrases may disclose hypocrisy, a sin that Jesus most vehemently condemned. (Conference Report, October 1951, p. 6.)

There are no blessings in supposedly good acts that are performed for the wrong reasons.

Errors and Transgressions

Motive is also important in the eternal significance assigned to acts that have bad consequences. Harmful acts can be committed with or without evil intent. Serious physical injuries can be inflicted by an intentional blow or a careless one. Words that inflict pain can be spoken with intent to hurt or simply through carelessness. The degree of moral evil in an act that injures another person is dependent upon the intent or motive of the actor. The scriptures reflect this principle by distinguishing between errors and transgressions.

The verb to err and the noun error are sometimes used as synonyms for transgression (see Alma 31:9; 37:8; D&C 6:11; 2 Peter 3:17). However, in other passages these words are used in the sense of an incorrect or mistaken action or inference (see 1 Nephi 19:6; Daniel 6:4). In this sense, to make an error is to do something inappropriate or incorrect but to do so without evil intent.

In the preface to the doctrines, covenants, and commandments given in this dispensation, the Lord revealed that his commandments were given to his servants "after the manner of their language, that they might come to understanding" (D&C 1:24). The verses that follow express a contrast between errors and sins:

> And inasmuch as they erred it might be made known;
> And inasmuch as they sought wisdom they might be instructed;
> And inasmuch as they sinned they might be chastened, that they might repent. (D&C 1:25–27; italics added.)

In succeeding verses the Lord declares that men should "repent" because he "cannot look upon sin with the least degree of allowance" (D&C 1:31–32).

The implication of these verses is that if we have "erred"—that is, if we have failed to act or acted incorrectly but have done so without wrongful intent—our error will be "made known" and we will thereby be taught correct behavior. In contrast, if we have "sinned," we will be "chastened" that we might make the necessary repen-

> John poses the ultimate challenge for the act of
> Christian love—that it not be merely in deeds or in
> words, but that it be in deeds done for pure motives.
> If we do this, the Apostle explains, we "shall assure
> our hearts before him." When our motives are right,
> and God knows this, our actions are acceptable to
> him. Then we will have what John calls "confidence
> toward God."

tance. Thus, errors merit correction, whereas sins require chastening and repentance. (See also D&C 20:80.)

The difference between errors and transgressions turns on the state of mind (or motive) with which we acted or failed to act. President Howard W. Hunter described this same difference when he said: "We should remember that errors of judgment are generally less serious than errors of intent" ("Parents' Concern for Children," *Ensign*, November 1983, p. 64).

In Deed and in Truth

"All things which are good cometh of God" (Moroni 7:12). In contrast, those things which only *seem* to be good —including acts that are done without real intent—are not necessarily of God and do not qualify to be blessed of him. The Apostle John applies this principle in his great message on our duty, as "sons of God," to "love one another" (1 John 3:2, 11). "My little children, let us not love in word, neither in tongue; but in deed and in truth" (1 John 3:18).

John poses the ultimate challenge for the act of Christian love—that it not be merely in deeds or in words, but that it be in deeds done for pure motives. If we do this, the Apostle explains, we "shall assure our hearts before him"

(1 John 3:19). When our motives are right, and God knows this, our actions are acceptable to him. Then we will have what John calls "confidence toward God":

> For if our heart condemn us, God is greater than our heart, and knoweth all things.
> Beloved, if our heart condemn us not, then have we confidence toward God. (1 John 3:20–21.)

The servant who does what is right and who acts for the right reasons has confidence in his or her relationship with the Creator. We should all strive for that confidence.

CHAPTER THREE

WHY WE SERVE

Service is an imperative for true followers of Jesus Christ. When his chosen leaders vied for prominent positions in his kingdom, the Savior cautioned them and then taught this great principle of leadership: "Whosoever will be chief among you, let him be your servant" (Matthew 20:27; see also Mark 10:35–45; Luke 22:24–27). On a later occasion he described how they should minister to the needs of the hungry, the naked, the sick, and the imprisoned. He concluded that teaching with these words: "Verily I say unto you, Inasmuch as ye have done it unto one of the least of these my brethren, ye have done it unto me" (Matthew 25:40).

In modern revelation the Lord has commanded that we "succor the weak, lift up the hands which hang down, and strengthen the feeble knees" (D&C 81:5). He has also instructed us to be "anxiously engaged in a good cause, and do many things of [our] own free will, and bring to pass much righteousness" (D&C 58:27). Holders of the

37

In modern revelation the Lord has instructed us to be
"anxiously engaged in a good cause, and do many
things of [our] own free will, and bring to pass much
righteousness." Holders of the Melchizedek
Priesthood receive it upon a covenant to use its powers
in the service of others. Indeed, service is a covenant
obligation of all members of the Church of Jesus
Christ.

Melchizedek Priesthood receive it upon a covenant to use
its powers in the service of others (see D&C 84:33–40).
Indeed, service is a covenant obligation of all members of
the Church of Jesus Christ.

Whether our service is to God or to our fellowmen, it is
the same. As King Benjamin testified to his people, "When
ye are in the service of your fellow beings ye are only in the
service of your God" (Mosiah 2:17). If we love him, we
should keep his commandments and feed his sheep (see
John 21:16–17).

When we think of service, we usually think of the acts
of our hands. But, as shown in earlier chapters, the Lord
looks to our hearts as well as our hands. He is concerned
not only with our acts but also with our motives. One of his
earliest commandments to Israel was to "love the Lord
your God, and to serve him with all your heart and with all
your soul" (Deuteronomy 11:13).

In order to purify our service to God and to our fellowmen, it is therefore important to consider not only *how* we
serve, but also *why* we serve.

People serve one another for different reasons, and
some reasons are better than others. It has been said that
"the biggest gap in the world is the gap between the justice
of a cause and the motives of the people pushing it" (John

P. Grier, in Lawrence J. Peter, comp., *Peter's Quotations*, [New York: William Morrow and Co., 1977], p. 340).

Perhaps none of us serves in every capacity all the time for only a single reason. Since we are imperfect beings, most of us probably serve for a combination of reasons. These combinations may be different from time to time as we grow spiritually. But we should all strive to serve for the reasons that are highest and best.

This chapter will discuss six reasons for service, presented in ascending order from the lesser to the greater. These six reasons are not exhaustive, but they are sufficient to illustrate and teach important contrasts and principles.

1. Earthly Reward

Some serve for hope of earthly reward. Such a man or woman may serve in a Church position or in private acts of mercy in an effort to achieve prominence or cultivate contacts that will increase income or aid in acquiring wealth. Others may serve in order to obtain worldly honors, prominence, or power.

Such motives are not new. In the meridian of time the chief Apostle exhorted the elders not to feed the flock for selfish personal reasons:

> Feed the flock of God which is among you, taking the oversight thereof, not by constraint, but willingly; not for filthy lucre, but of a ready mind;
> Neither as being lords over God's heritage, but being ensamples to the flock. (1 Peter 5:2–3.)

The scriptural word for gospel service "for the sake of riches and honor" is *priestcraft* (Alma 1:16). As noted in chapter 2, "priestcrafts are that men preach and set themselves up for a light unto the world, that they may get gain

Service that is ostensibly for God or fellowmen but is
really for the sake of the server's riches or honor
surely comes within the Savior's condemnation of
those who "outwardly appear righteous unto men, but
within . . . are full of hypocrisy and iniquity." Such
service earns no gospel reward.

---

and praise of the world" (2 Nephi 26:29). We see a signal
mark of spiritual deterioration in the Book of Mormon in
those times when the people "began to build up churches
unto themselves to get gain" (4 Nephi 1:26; see also Mormon 8:33). In modern revelation the Lord has again condemned "priestcrafts" (D&C 33:4) and the corruption of
religion by "build[ing] up churches unto themselves to get
gain" (D&C 10:56).

In these latter days we are commanded to "seek to
bring forth and establish the cause of Zion" (D&C 6:6).
Unfortunately, not all who accomplish works under that
heading are really intending to build up Zion or to
strengthen the faith of the people of God. Other motives
can be at work.

Service that is ostensibly for God or fellowmen but is
really for the sake of the server's riches or honor surely
comes within the Savior's condemnation of those who
"outwardly appear righteous unto men, but within . . .
are full of hypocrisy and iniquity" (Matthew 23:28). Such
service earns no gospel reward. All Latter-day Saints
should remember Nephi's warning: "But the laborer in
Zion shall labor for Zion; for if they labor for money they
shall perish" (2 Nephi 26:31).

In contrast to those who complete their service for selfish reasons, such as to be seen of men, those who serve
quietly, even "in secret," qualify for the Savior's promise

that "thy Father who seeth in secret, himself shall reward thee openly" (3 Nephi 13:4; Matthew 6:4).

2. Good Companionship

Another reason for service—probably more worthy than the first but still in the category of service in search of earthly reward—is that which is motivated by a desire to obtain good companionship. We surely have good associations in our Church service, but is that an acceptable motive for service?

I knew a person who was active in Church service until a socially prominent friend and fellow worker moved away. When the friend moved from the ward, this person ceased to serve. This worker was only willing to serve when he found the fellow workers acceptable.

Persons who serve only to obtain good companionship are more selective in choosing their friends than the Master was in choosing his servants. Jesus called most of his servants from those in humble circumstances. And he associated with sinners. He answered the critics of such associations by saying: "They that are whole need not a physician; but they that are sick. I came not to call the righteous, but sinners to repentance." (Luke 5:31–32.)

The first section of the Doctrine and Covenants, which prophesies of people in the last days, gives a description of those "who will not hear the voice of the Lord, neither the voice of his servants" (D&C 1:14). This description seems to include those who serve for hope of earthly reward of one sort or another:

> They seek not the Lord to establish his righteousness, but every man walketh in his own way, and after the image of his own god, whose image is in the likeness of the world, and whose substance is that of an idol. (D&C 1:16.)

41

These first two reasons for service are obviously selfish and self-serving and unworthy of Saints. Reasons aimed at earthly compensations are distinctly inferior in character and reward.

3. Fear of Punishment

Some serve out of fear of punishment. The scriptures abound with descriptions of the miserable state of those who fail to follow the commandments of God.

The Savior described what will happen when the Son of Man comes in his glory and gathers all nations before him for judgment (see Matthew 25:31–32). To those who have not sheltered and clothed the stranger, administered to the needs of the hungry and thirsty, and visited those who are sick and in prison, he will say: "Depart from me, ye cursed, into everlasting fire, prepared for the devil and his angels" (Matthew 25:41).

In addition, King Benjamin taught his people that the soul of the rebellious and unrepentant transgressor would be filled with

> a lively sense of his own guilt, which doth cause him to shrink from the presence of the Lord, and doth fill his breast with guilt, and pain, and anguish, which is like an unquenchable fire, whose flame ascendeth up forever and ever (Mosiah 2:38).

These descriptions surely offer sufficient incentive for keeping the commandment of service. But service out of fear of punishment is a lesser motive at best.

4. Duty or Loyalty

Other persons serve out of a sense of duty or out of loyalty to family, friends, or traditions. I would call such persons "good soldiers." They instinctively do what they are asked, without question, and sometimes without giving much thought to the reasons for their service. Such persons fill the ranks of voluntary organizations everywhere, and they do much good. We have all benefited from their good works. Those who serve out of a sense of duty or out of loyalty to various wholesome causes are the good and honorable men and women of the earth.

Service of this character is worthy of praise and will surely qualify for blessings, especially if it is done willingly and joyfully. As the Apostle Paul wrote in his second letter to the Corinthians:

> But this I say, He which soweth sparingly shall reap also sparingly; and he which soweth bountifully shall reap also bountifully.
>
> Every man according as he purposeth in his heart, so let him give; not grudgingly, or of necessity: for God loveth a cheerful giver. (2 Corinthians 9:6–7.)

"It is obeying God willingly that is accepted," an anonymous writer has said. "The Lord hates that which is forced. It is rather a tax than an offering."

Although those who serve out of fear of punishment or out of a sense of duty undoubtedly qualify for the blessings of heaven, there are still higher reasons for service.

5. Hope of Reward

One such higher reason for service is the hope of an eternal reward. This hope—the expectation of eventually enjoying the fruits of our labors—is one of our most powerful motivations. The prophet Helaman used this motivation successfully as he taught his sons, Nephi and Lehi. Years later, in their adult years, these stalwart servants of the Lord remembered their father's teaching that it was not only important for them to "do that which is good," but to do it for the right reasons. Helaman taught his sons that

43

they should not do that which is good "that ye may boast, but that ye may do these things to lay up for yourselves a treasure in heaven, yea, which is eternal" (Helaman 5:7–8).

In his great prophecy of the final judgment the Savior foretold that the King would set the sheep on his right hand:

> Then shall the King say unto them on his right hand, Come, ye blessed of my Father, inherit the kingdom prepared for you from the foundation of the world:
>
> For I was an hungred, and ye gave me meat: I was thirsty, and ye gave me drink; I was a stranger, and ye took me in:
>
> Naked, and ye clothed me: I was sick, and ye visited me: I was in prison, and ye came unto me. . . .
>
> Verily I say unto you, Inasmuch as ye have done it unto one of the least of these my brethren, ye have done it unto me. (Matthew 25:34–36, 40.)

Hope of eternal reward is an acceptable motive. As a reason for service, it necessarily involves faith in God and trust in the fulfillment of his prophecies and promises.

The scriptures are rich in promises of eternal rewards for those who serve God and keep his commandments. For example, the third chapter of Malachi, which the Savior quoted to the Nephites after his resurrection (3 Nephi 24), contains this promise:

> Ye have said, It is vain to serve God: and what profit is it that we have kept his ordinance, and that we have walked mournfully before the Lord of hosts?
>
> And now we call the proud happy; yea, they that work wickedness are set up; yea, they that tempt God are even delivered.
>
> Then they that feared the Lord spake often one to another: and the Lord hearkened, and heard it, and a book of remembrance was written before him for them that feared the Lord, and that thought upon his name.

Whenever we focus on ourselves, even in our service to others, we fall short of the example of our Savior, who gave himself as a total and unqualified sacrifice for all mankind. Those who seek to follow his example must lose themselves in their service to others.

And they shall be mine, saith the Lord of hosts, in that day when I make up my jewels; and I will spare them, as a man spareth his own son that serveth him.

Then shall ye return, and discern between the righteous and the wicked, between him that serveth God and him that serveth him not. (Malachi 3:14–18.)

In addition to the other promises quoted above, we have the revelation given through the Prophet Joseph Smith in June 1829, in which the Lord said: "If you keep my commandments and endure to the end you shall have eternal life, which gift is the greatest of all the gifts of God" (D&C 14:7).

The above five motives for service have a common deficiency. In varying degrees each focuses on the actor's personal advantage, either on earth or in the judgment to follow. Each is self-centered.

There is something deficient about any service that is conscious of self. A few months after my calling to the Council of the Twelve, I expressed my feelings of inadequacy to one of the senior members of my quorum. He responded with this mild reproof and challenging insight: "I suppose your feelings are understandable. But you should work for a condition where you will not be preoccupied with yourself and your own feelings and can give your entire concern to others, to the work of the Lord in all the world."

Whenever we focus on ourselves, even in our service to others, we fall short of the example of our Savior, who gave himself as a total and unqualified sacrifice for all mankind. Those who seek to follow his example must lose themselves in their service to others.

Elder Thomas S. Monson taught this principle in a sermon on the special blessings of loving service anonymously given. He illustrated the principle with Henry Van Dyke's classic, "The Mansion," which describes the heavenly vision of John Weightman, prominent philanthropist. This man, who had liked to put his gifts "where they can be identified," was astonished at the insignificance of his heavenly mansion. "Have you not heard that I have built a schoolhouse; a wing of a hospital?" he asked his guide. The guide replied:

> "They were not ill done. But they were all marked and used as foundations for the name and mansion of John Weightman in the world. . . . Verily, you have had your reward for them. Would you be paid twice?"
>
> A sadder but wiser John Weightman spoke more humbly: "What is it that counts here?"
>
> Came the reply, "Only that which is truly given. Only that good which is done for the love of doing it. Only those plans in which the welfare of others is the master thought. Only those labors in which the sacrifice is greater than the reward. Only those gifts in which the giver forgets himself." ("The Mansion" in *Unknown Quantity: A Book of Romance and Some Half-told Tales* [New York: Scribner's, 1918], pp. 364–68.)

Elder Monson concluded:

> May this truth guide our lives. May we look upward as we press forward in the service of our God and our fellowmen. And may we incline an ear toward Galilee, that we might hear perhaps an echo of the Savior's teachings: "Do not your alms before men, to be seen of them." (Matthew 6:1.) "Let

not thy left hand know what thy right hand doeth." (Matthew 6:3.) And of our good deeds: "See thou tell no man." (Matthew 8:4.) Our hearts will then be lighter, our lives brighter, and our souls richer.

Loving service anonymously given may be unknown to man—but the gift and the giver are known to God. ("Anonymous," *Ensign*, May 1983, p. 57.)

6. Charity

The sixth reason for service is the highest of all. It is what the Apostle Paul called "a more excellent way" (1 Corinthians 12:31).

Charity is "the pure love of Christ" (Moroni 7:47). The Book of Mormon teaches us that this virtue is "the greatest of all" (Moroni 7:46). "And except ye have charity ye can in nowise be saved in the kingdom of God" (Moroni 10:21). Paul affirmed and illustrated that truth in his great teaching about the reasons for service:

> Though I speak with the tongues of men and of angels, and have not charity, I am become as sounding brass, or a tinkling cymbal.
>
> And though I have the gift of prophecy, and understand all mysteries, and all knowledge; and though I have all faith, so that I could remove mountains, and have not charity, I am nothing.
>
> And though I bestow all my goods to feed the poor, and though I give my body to be burned, and have not charity, it profiteth me nothing. (1 Corinthians 13:1–3.)

We know from these inspired words that even the most extreme acts of service fall short of the ultimate "profit" unless they are motivated by the pure love of Christ.

If our service is to be most efficacious, it must be unconcerned with self and heedless of personal advantage. It must be accomplished for the love of God and the love of

It is not enough to serve God with all of our might and strength. He who looks into our hearts and knows our minds demands more than this. In order to stand blameless before God at the last day, we must also serve him with all our heart and mind.

---

his children. The Savior applied that principle in the Sermon on the Mount, wherein he commanded us to love our enemies, bless them that curse us, do good to them that hate us, and pray for them that despitefully use us and persecute us (see Matthew 5:44; 3 Nephi 12:44). He explained the purpose of that commandment as follows:

> For if ye love them which love you, what reward have ye? do not even the publicans the same?
> And if ye salute your brethren only, what do ye more than others? do not even the publicans so? (Matthew 5:46–47).

This principle—that our service should be for the love of God and the love of fellowmen rather than for personal advantage or any other lesser motive—is admittedly a high standard. The Savior must have seen it so, since he joined this commandment of selfless and complete love directly to the ideal of perfection. The very next verse of the Sermon on the Mount contains this great command: "Be ye therefore perfect, even as your Father which is in heaven is perfect" (Matthew 5:48; see also 3 Nephi 12:48).

This principle of service is reaffirmed in the fourth section of the Doctrine and Covenants:

> Therefore, O ye that embark in the service of God, see that ye serve him with all your heart, might, mind and strength, that ye may stand blameless before God at the last day (D&C 4:2).

Here we learn that it is not enough to serve God with all of our *might and strength*. He who looks into our hearts and knows our minds demands more than this. In order to stand blameless before God at the last day, we must also serve him with all our *heart and mind.*

Self-effacing service with all of our heart and mind is a high challenge for all of us. Such service must be motivated solely by the pure love of Christ. Those who forget themselves and give service in this manner can look up to God "with a pure heart and clean hands" (Alma 5:19).

CHAPTER FOUR

DESIRES WITHOUT ACTIONS

We are accountable for our desires, independent of our actions.
Desire is a state of mind that craves or wishes for something. Desires shape our motives, why we act, and what we wish to accomplish by our actions. Our most basic desires fix our priorities and identify our purpose in life.

We are accustomed to thinking that our actions make us what we are. But since our actions are stimulated by our desires, it is more accurate to say that our desires make us what we are. Bruce C. Hafen said it well:

> Not only will the righteous desires of our hearts be granted, but also the unrighteous desires of our hearts. Over the long run, our most deeply held desires will govern our choices, one by one and day by day, until our lives finally add up to what we have really wanted. (*The Believing Heart* [Salt Lake City: Bookcraft, 1986], p. 26.)

Remarking upon the power of our desires, another writer predicted: "You will become as small as your controlling

51

**"The nearer man approaches perfection, the clearer
are his views, and the greater his enjoyments, till he
has overcome the evils of his life and lost every desire
for sin; and like the ancients, arrives at that point of
faith where he is wrapped in the power and glory of
his Maker, and is caught up to dwell with Him."**

---

desire; as great as your dominant aspiration" (James
Allen, *As a Man Thinketh* [Salt Lake City: Bookcraft,
n.d.], p. 55).

Abraham's life illustrates this principle. As he recorded:

> I sought for the blessings of the fathers, . . . desiring also to
> be one who possessed great knowledge and to be a greater
> follower of righteousness, . . . and desiring to receive in-
> structions, and to keep the commandments of God.

In consequence of these desires, Abraham "became a
rightful heir, a High Priest, holding the right belonging to
the fathers" (Abraham 1:2).

The Prophet Joseph Smith taught that on the way to
perfection we must lose "every desire for sin."

> The nearer man approaches perfection, the clearer are his
> views, and the greater his enjoyments, till he has overcome
> the evils of his life and lost every desire for sin; and like the
> ancients, arrives at that point of faith where he is wrapped in
> the power and glory of his Maker, and is caught up to dwell
> with Him (*History of the Church* 2:8).

Desires in the Judgment

We will be judged on the basis of our desires. In modern
revelation the Lord explained, "For I, the Lord, will judge
all men according to their works, according to the desire of
their hearts" (D&C 137:9).

The prophet Alma taught that when we are "brought before the bar of God, to be judged," our "works" will condemn us, "and our thoughts will also condemn us" (Alma 12:12, 14). When Alma explained this principle to his wayward son, Corianton, he called it "the plan of restoration [which] is requisite with the justice of God" (Alma 41:2):

> And it is requisite with the justice of God that men should be judged according to their works; and if their works were good in this life, and the desires of their hearts were good, that they should also, at the last day, be restored unto that which is good.
>
> And if their works are evil they shall be restored unto them for evil. Therefore, all things shall be restored to their proper order, every thing to its natural frame. (Alma 41:3–4.)

Further stressing the importance of desire, Alma repeated the principle in these words:

> The one raised to happiness according to his desires of happiness, or good according to his desires of good; and the other to evil according to his desires of evil; for as he has desired to do evil all the day long even so shall he have his reward of evil when the night cometh.
>
> And so it is on the other hand. If he hath repented of his sins, and desired righteousness until the end of his days, even so he shall be rewarded unto righteousness. (Alma 41:5–6; see also Alma 29:5.)

We will be judged for what we are. As Alma explains:

> The meaning of the word restoration is to bring back again evil for evil, or carnal for carnal, or devilish for devilish— good for that which is good; righteous for that which is righteous; just for that which is just; merciful for that which is merciful (Alma 41:13).

Alma's counsel to Corianton ends with his great exposition of justice and mercy, which concludes with this re-emphasis of the importance of deeds *and* desires:

Therefore, O my son, whosoever will come may come and partake of the waters of life freely; and whosoever will not come the same is not compelled to come; but in the last day it shall be restored unto him according to his *deeds.*

If he has *desired* to do evil, and has not repented in his days, behold, evil shall be done unto him, according to the restoration of God. (Alma 42:27–28; italics added.)

Evil Desires

The scriptures contain many commands to avoid evil desires. For example, latter-day revelations identify telestial wickedness not only in he who "makes a lie" but also in he who "loves" a lie (D&C 76:103; 63:17).

"Thou shalt not covet" (Exodus 20:17) is clearly a command addressed to a state of mind rather than to an action. In modern times the Lord reemphasized this principle by commanding the Saints to cease from their "lustful desires, from all [their] pride and light-mindedness" (D&C 88:121), and to repent "of all their covetous desires, before me, . . . for what is property unto me? saith the Lord" (D&C 117:4).

Despite these commands, there are many whose desires are fixed so firmly on the acquisition or use of property, or on other worldly things, that they have no desire for righteousness or the things of God.

In the parable of the sower, Jesus indicated that some of the sower's seed "fell by the way side" (Matthew 13:4). He explained to his disciples that this circumstance represented those who "heareth the word of the kingdom, and understandeth it not" (Matthew 13:19). The Prophet Joseph Smith attributed this lack of understanding of the gospel to a lack of desire:

Men who have no principle of righteousness in themselves, and whose hearts are full of iniquity, and have no desire for

The Book of Mormon declares that God's people in an earlier day "despised the words of plainness, and killed the prophets, and sought for things that they could not understand." Then and now, some people prefer an obscure philosophy or a complicated theory to the simple principles of revealed truth. Then and now, we are likely to value and to receive what we desire.

---

the principles of truth, do not understand the word of truth when they hear it. The devil taketh away the word of truth out of their hearts, because there is no desire for righteousness in them. (*History of the Church* 2:266.)

The seeds representing the word of God will always fall "by the way side" for those who give their priority attention to traffic on the highway of worldly things. If there is no *desire* for the principles of truth, the seed that represents the word of God can never bear fruit.

Similarly, if we do not desire to have the principles of the gospel taught in words of plainness, we may be granted our desire. The Book of Mormon declares that God's people in an earlier day "despised the words of plainness, and killed the prophets, and sought for things that they could not understand." Then and now, some people prefer an obscure philosophy or a complicated theory to the simple principles of revealed truth. Then and now, we are likely to value and to receive what we desire. "Wherefore, . . . they must needs fall; for God hath taken away his plainness from them, and delivered unto them many things which they cannot understand, because they desired it." (Jacob 4:14.)

The New Testament and the Book of Mormon contain many other examples of the Savior's concern with thoughts and desires. In the Sermon on the Mount, he gave this teaching about anger:

> Ye have heard that it was said by them of old time, Thou shalt not kill; and whosoever shall kill shall be in danger of the judgment:
> But I say unto you, That whosoever is angry with his brother without a cause shall be in danger of the judgment. (Matthew 5:21–22; see also 3 Nephi 12:21–22, which omits the qualification "without a cause.")

Better known is the Savior's teaching about sexual sin:

> Ye have heard that it was said by them of old time, Thou shalt not commit adultery:
> But I say unto you, That whosoever looketh on a woman to lust after her hath committed adultery with her already in his heart. (Matthew 5:27–28.)

After recording the same teaching in virtually identical phraseology (3 Nephi 12:27–28), the Book of Mormon records this significant conclusion to the Savior's teachings on anger and lust:

> Behold, I give unto you a commandment, that ye suffer none of these things to enter into your heart (3 Nephi 12:29).

This same principle applies to feelings of hatred. Elder Bruce R. McConkie writes: "It is the feeling one has in his heart that counts, not the eventuality that occurs. 'Whosoever hateth his brother is a murderer: and ye know that no murderer hath eternal life abiding in him' " (1 John 3:15) (*The Mortal Messiah* [Salt Lake City: Deseret Book Co., 1980], 2:135).

We should not only avoid hateful and lustful designs focused upon specific persons. We should also refrain from approving evil, and we should even avoid the most general thoughts of it. As Jacob taught, those who inherit the kingdom of God are those "who have endured the crosses of

What does it mean to "envy sinners"? We do this if we envy those who seem to have pleasure in violating the commandments, such as by gambling or by patronizing commercial amusements on the Sabbath. More generally, we envy sinners if we wish we had never been taught the truth or had never made covenants, so we could sin with impunity. We envy sinners whenever we long to participate in conduct we know to be forbidden.

---

the world, and despised the shame of it" (2 Nephi 9:18). The author of Proverbs expressed the commandment in this way: "Let not thine heart envy sinners: but be thou in the fear of the Lord all the day long" (Proverbs 23:17).

What does it mean to "envy sinners"? We do this if we envy those who seem to have pleasure in violating the commandments, such as by gambling or by patronizing commercial amusements on the Sabbath. More generally, we envy sinners if we wish we had never been taught the truth or had never made covenants, so we could sin with impunity. We envy sinners whenever we long to participate in conduct we know to be forbidden.

In praising charity, the Apostle Paul declared that charity "thinketh no evil; rejoiceth not in iniquity, but rejoiceth in the truth" (1 Corinthians 13:5–6; see also Moroni 7:45). Similarly, the prophet Moroni warned those who "despise the works of the Lord" (Mormon 9:26).

What does it mean to "despise the works of the Lord" or to "rejoice in iniquity"? This must include those who ridicule the Lord's Church or its work. It must also include those who poke fun at persons who are striving to do what is right, or those who applaud wickedness even though they do not participate in it.

Most of us have seen such ridicule many times. For example, I knew an elderly woman who was sweet and trusting—some would say naive. After she found a twenty-dollar bill on a busy sidewalk, she immediately began stopping pedestrians to ask if they had lost it. Inevitably she met the cunning man who did not hesitate to lie for gain. She innocently delivered the bill to him and went her way rejoicing in her good deed. He later bragged about how he had tricked "that dumb old woman." Those who joined in laughter at her expense or implied their approval of his conduct "rejoiced in iniquity."

In our own dispensation the Lord called rebellious Saints to repentance because they "have pleasure in unrighteousness" (D&C 56:15). One form of pleasure in unrighteousness is the continued surrender to habits that violate commandments, such as indulgence in tobacco or habit-forming drugs. Elder M. Russell Ballard has suggested why it is vital to overcome such habits and desires while we are in mortality:

> If you have a bad habit, do you think death is going to change it? Do you think that habit will simply dissolve in some miraculous way and will no longer be with you? I believe that the Lord impresses upon you and me the need to repent and live the law, keep the commandments, and keep our lives aligned to the celestial goal; because it is when we are here in mortality that the body and the spirit can learn together.
>
> For example, when a man who smokes dies and his body is placed six feet into the ground, is there any reason for us to believe that when his body comes back up out of the ground it will no longer have the desires that it had when it was laid down? I do not think so. I think that the body will rise in the resurrection with the same desires and that the body and the spirit together must work out this matter of eternal salvation. (B.Y.U. Speeches of the Year, 1979, pp. 157–8.)

This principle means that when we have done all that we can, our desires will carry us the rest of the way. It also means that if our desires are right, we can be forgiven for the unintended errors or mistakes we will inevitably make as we try to carry those desires into effect. What a comfort for our feelings of inadequacy!

These are warnings to all Latter-day Saints who think themselves justified when they refrain from evil acts, but still indulge themselves in evil thoughts and desires.

Righteous Desires

Just as we will be accountable for our evil desires, we will also be rewarded for our righteous ones. Our Father in Heaven will receive a truly righteous desire as a substitute for actions that are genuinely impossible. My father-in-law was fond of expressing his version of this principle. When someone wanted to do something for him but was prevented by circumstances, he would say: "Thank you. I will take the good will for the deed."

This is the principle that blessed Abraham for his willingness to sacrifice his son Isaac. The Lord stopped him at the last instant (see Genesis 22:11–12), but his willingness to follow the Lord's command "was accounted unto him for righteousness" (D&C 132:36).

This principle means that when we have *done* all that we can, our *desires* will carry us the rest of the way. It also means that if our desires are right, we can be forgiven for the unintended errors or mistakes we will inevitably make as we try to carry those desires into effect. What a comfort for our feelings of inadequacy!

President Brigham Young expressed this comforting assurance in a sermon he gave in 1857:

> No matter what the outward appearance is—if I can know of a truth that the hearts of the people are fully set to do the will of their Father in heaven, though they may falter and do a great many things through the weaknesses of human nature, yet, they will be saved. . . .
>
> If their motives are pure—no matter whether their outward appearance is particularly precise, their acts will be discerned by the Spirit of the Lord, and will be appreciated for what they were intended. If people act from pure motives, though their outward movements may not always be so pleasant as our traditions would prefer, yet God will make those acts result in the best good to the people. (*Journal of Discourses* 5:256.)

A man who had been excommunicated from the Church wrote to me from a prison where he had spent the previous eleven years. His letter described the "enormous sense of comfort" he had received from the assurance that we will be rewarded for the desires of our hearts. "Of all the many directions my life has taken," he wrote, "none has been more satisfying than the day I let the light of Christ enter my life." With that light he proceeded with his repentance and acquired what he called a "burning desire to do my part for the cause of Zion." Writing from a prison, where he was "limited in movement and association," he nevertheless felt comfort "to know that my desires will be counted for good."

There are many kinds of prisons in this life—many limits on movement, association, and other actions. The principle that we will be rewarded for our desires notwithstanding our inability to act offers comfort in all of these circumstances.

The most detailed scriptural illustration of an assured reward for an unfulfilled desire is King Benjamin's teaching about giving:

And again, I say unto the poor . . . all you who deny the beggar, because ye have not; I would that ye say in your hearts that: I give not because I have not, but if I had I would give.

And now, if ye say this in your hearts ye remain guiltless. (Mosiah 4:24–25.)

Paul described the same principle in his second letter to the Corinthians, in which he said, "If there be first a willing mind, it is accepted according to that a man hath, and not according to that he hath not" (2 Corinthians 8:12). What a contrast between these examples and those of the priest and the Levite, who looked on the wounded man but "passed by on the other side of the way; for they desired in their hearts that it might not be known that they had seen him" (JST Luke 10:33).

President Harold B. Lee relied on the above scriptures on the desire to give when he defined another example of rewards for righteous desires:

[Women] who have been denied the blessings of wifehood or motherhood in this life—who say in their heart, if I could have done, I would have done, or I would give if I had, but I cannot, for I have not—the Lord will bless you as though you had done, and the world to come will compensate for those who desire in their hearts the righteous blessings that they were not able to have because of no fault of their own. (*Ye Are the Light of the World* [Salt Lake City: Deseret Book Co., 1974], p. 292.)

In his famous tithing sermon in St. George in May 1899, President Lorenzo Snow also directed this promise to a group of unmarried sisters who were questioning what their condition would be in the next life:

I desire to give a little explanation for the comfort and consolation of parties in this condition. There is no Latter-day Saint who dies after having lived a faithful life who will lose anything because of having failed to do certain things when

"In the great plan of salvation nothing has been overlooked. The gospel of Jesus Christ is the most beautiful thing in the world. It embraces every soul whose heart is right and who diligently seeks him and desires to obey his laws and covenants. Therefore, if a person is for any cause denied the privilege of complying with any of the covenants, the Lord will judge him or her by the intent of the heart."

---

opportunities were not furnished him or her. In other words, if a young man or a young woman has no opportunity of getting married, and they live faithful lives up to the time of their death, they will have all the blessings, exaltation and glory that any man or woman will have who had this opportunity and improved it. . . . People who have no opportunity of marrying in this life, if they die in the Lord, will have means furnished them by which they can secure all the blessings necessary for persons in the married condition. (*Millennial Star,* August 31, 1899, p. 547.)

Elder Joseph Fielding Smith repeated this promise to the unmarried and the childless, and then gave this explanation of the principle upon which the prophetic assurance is based:

In the great plan of salvation nothing has been overlooked. The gospel of Jesus Christ is the most beautiful thing in the world. It embraces every soul whose heart is right and who diligently seeks him and desires to obey his laws and covenants. Therefore, if a person is for any cause denied the privilege of complying with any of the covenants, the Lord will judge him or her by the intent of the heart. (*Selections from* Answers to Gospel Questions, *Course of Study for Melchizedek Priesthood Quorums, 1972–73,* pp. 267–68.)

The requirement for entry into the celestial kingdom is not that we have actually practiced the entire celestial law while upon this earth, but that we have shown God that we are willing and able to do so. Many have lived in ages of the world when they were not even taught the full celestial law. In our day the Lord has said this about such people:

> All who have died without a knowledge of this gospel, who would have received it if they had been permitted to tarry, shall be heirs of the celestial kingdom of God;
>
> Also all that shall die henceforth without a knowledge of it, who would have received it with all their hearts, shall be heirs of that kingdom. (D&C 137:7–8.)

What does it mean to be an "heir" of the celestial kingdom? An heir is one who has a rightful claim to an inheritance. But his inheritance is not automatic. An heir must perfect his claim by complying with certain formalities. In the secular law, these formalities include such requirements as filing a proof of heirship within the required time and showing that all the debts of the estate are paid. In the gospel law, the formalities include the required ordinances of the gospel, as discussed later.

Modern revelation states that "he who is not able to abide the law of a celestial kingdom cannot abide a celestial glory" (D&C 88:22). This implies that he who *is* "able" to abide the law of a celestial kingdom will be an heir of the celestial kingdom. "In other words," Elder McConkie explains, "salvation in the celestial kingdom will come to all who are *able* to live the full law of Christ, even though they did not have opportunity so to do in the course of a mortal probation" (*The Mortal Messiah*, 1:74).

Perhaps this principle explains the parable of the rich man and Lazarus (Luke 16:19–31). Though in this life "full of sores" and pitiable in his poverty, the beggar Lazarus was worthy at death to be "carried by the angels into Abraham's bosom," for which he was envied by the rich man. The beggar must have been exceedingly limited in the *acts* he could perform during life, but he must have made great spiritual progress because of the *desires of his heart*.

Elder Neal A. Maxwell offered a related insight:

> The rickshaw wallah of Calcutta who refuses to beg, who instead runs for ten hours a day in order to help his family barely survive, will carry all of his self-discipline and meekness with him into the next world, bringing it to bear on his greatly enlarged opportunities there. (*But for a Small Moment* [Salt Lake City: Bookcraft, 1986], p. 99.)

The Book of Mormon contains many illustrations of the principle that we can make spiritual progress by righteous thoughts and desires.

Alma the Younger went about with the sons of Mosiah, seeking to destroy the Church (Mosiah 27). He was stricken by an angel of God, and for three days and nights lay helpless, "racked with eternal torment . . . tormented with the pains of hell" (Alma 36:12–13, 16). He was not restored by any act on his part, or even by any act or words of blessing from his worthy and anxious father. As he told his own son Helaman many years later, what brought Alma relief was the desire of his heart to draw close to his Savior:

> And it came to pass that as I was thus racked with torment, while I was harrowed up by the memory of my many sins, behold, I remembered also to have heard my father prophesy unto the people concerning the coming of one Jesus Christ, a Son of God, to atone for the sins of the world.
>
> Now, as my mind caught hold upon this thought, I cried within my heart: O Jesus, thou Son of God, have mercy on me, who am in the gall of bitterness, and am encircled about by the everlasting chains of death.
>
> And now, behold, when I thought this, I could remember my pains no more; yea, I was harrowed up by the memory of my sins no more.

Hardships can deprive mortals of the power to act. But at the same time, hardships can be the means of eternal growth in attitude and desire. If endured with the right attitude and accompanied by righteous desires, suffering and deprivation can be the agency of great growth in our spirits.

And oh, what joy, and what marvelous light I did behold; yea, my soul was filled with joy as exceeding as was my pain! (Alma 36:17–20.)

In his great sermon to the Zoramites, Alma explained the principle that our desires can shape our souls:

But behold, if ye will awake and arouse your faculties, even to an experiment upon my words, and exercise a particle of faith, yea, even if ye can no more than desire to believe, let this desire work in you, even until ye believe in a manner that ye can give place for a portion of my words (Alma 32:27).

Alma then compared the word to a seed, which, if not cast out by unbelief, will begin to swell, to enlarge the soul, and to enlighten the understanding. If nourished, it will become a tree springing up unto everlasting life (Alma 32:28–41).

Hardships can deprive mortals of the power to *act*. But at the same time, hardships can be the means of eternal growth in *attitude and desire*. If endured with the right attitude and accompanied by righteous desires, suffering and deprivation can be the agency of great growth in our spirits.

Viktor E. Frankl describes this principle in his account of tragic experiences in a Nazi concentration camp. He concludes that no matter how much is taken away in human freedom, no matter how severe the persecutions, no matter how terrible the conditions of psychic and physical stress, man can preserve what Frankl calls "the last of the human freedoms—to choose one's attitude in any given set of circumstances, to choose one's own way." Frankl writes:

> Even though conditions such as lack of sleep, insufficient food and various mental stresses may suggest that the inmates were bound to react in certain ways, in the final analysis it becomes clear that the sort of person the prisoner became was the result of an inner decision, and not the result of camp influences alone. Fundamentally, therefore, any man can, even under such circumstances, decide what shall become of him—mentally and spiritually. . . . It is this spiritual freedom—which cannot be taken away—that makes life meaningful and purposeful.

> An active life serves the purpose of giving man the opportunity to realize values in creative work, while a passive life of enjoyment affords him the opportunity to obtain fulfillment in experiencing beauty, art, or nature. But there is also purpose in that life which is almost barren of both creation and enjoyment and which admits of but one possibility of high moral behavior: namely, in man's attitude to his existence, an existence restricted by external forces. A creative life and a life of enjoyment are banned to him. But not only creativeness and enjoyment are meaningful. If there is a meaning in life at all, then there must be a meaning in suffering. Suffering is an ineradicable part of life, even as fate and death. Without suffering and death human life cannot be complete.

> The way in which a man accepts his fate and all the suffering it entails, the way in which he takes up his cross, gives him ample opportunity—even under the most difficult circumstances—to add a deeper meaning to his life. (From *Man's Search for Meaning* by Viktor E. Frankl. Revised edition copyright © 1962 by Viktor Frankl. Reprinted by permission of Beacon Press.)

The Apostle Paul indicated that he was given "a thorn in the flesh" to buffet him, "lest I should be exalted above measure" (2 Corinthians 12:7). Three times he pleaded with the Lord to take it from him, but the Lord chose instead to explain its purpose: "And he said unto me, My grace is sufficient for thee: for my strength is made perfect in weakness" (2 Corinthians 12:9). Indeed, the weakness of the flesh—our inability to act with complete freedom—does not prevent us from perfecting the desires of our hearts, and in this way we can progress in the development of characteristics that are not bound to earth—the qualities of our eternal soul.

Persons who are deprived of sight, hearing, or movement, parents who care for a handicapped child, and persons who are compelled to endure conditions of economic hardship, political oppression, or even obnoxious personal associations, can achieve extraordinary spiritual growth through the process of coping with such adversities. God is just. He knows all things, and all things are present before his eyes (see D&C 38:2). When we can see our own condition and behavior as he sees them, we will understand why he told the imprisoned and suffering Prophet Joseph Smith, "all these things shall give thee experience, and shall be for thy good" (D&C 122:7).

Desires are vital. Righteous desires will be rewarded. The Lord promised his servants in this dispensation: "Verily, verily, I say unto you, even as you desire of me so it shall be unto you; and if you desire, you shall be the means of doing much good in this generation" (D&C 6:8; 11:8; see also D&C 7:8).

Some Cautions

Two cautions are necessary to those who would rely on this principle that we can qualify for blessings and growth without completing the acts usually required for them.

Desire is a substitute only when action is truly impossible. If we attempt to use impossibility of action as a cover (when we really lack a sincere desire to keep the commandment) and therefore do not do all that we can to perform the acts that have been commanded, we may deceive ourselves, but we will not deceive the Righteous Judge.

First, we must remember that desire is a substitute only when action is truly impossible. For example, suppose a person refrained from paying tithing in the thought that his desire to be a full tithepayer would meet the requirement. It will not. The payment of tithing can be difficult; but since it is required only when we have received income, it is rarely impossible. If we attempt to use impossibility of action as a cover (when we really lack a sincere desire to keep the commandment) and therefore do not do all that we can to perform the acts that have been commanded, we may deceive ourselves, but we will not deceive the Righteous Judge.

In order to serve as a substitute for action, desire cannot be superficial, impulsive, or temporary. It must be heartfelt, through and through. There is a persuasive analogy in the Apostle Paul's reference to the kind of sorrow necessary for repentance unto salvation. What he calls the "sorrow of the world" is insufficient. That sorrow "worketh death." Repentance requires what he calls "godly sorrow" (2 Corinthians 7:10). To be efficacious for blessings in lieu of required actions, the reasons for inaction must be so justified and the desires of our hearts must be so genuine that they too can be called godly.

An experience related by Elder Russell M. Nelson helps us understand the intensity of desire necessary to qualify for blessings on this basis:

I was with Elder Mark E. Petersen in the Holy Land in October 1983, during his last mortal journey. Elder Petersen was not well. Evidences of his consuming malignancy were so painfully real to him, yet he derived strength from the Savior he served. Following a night of intense suffering, aggravated by pangs of his progressive inability to eat or to drink, Elder Petersen addressed throngs assembled at the Mount of Beatitudes to hear his discourse on the "Sermon on the Mount." After he recited "Blessed are they which do hunger and thirst after righteousness," he departed from the biblical text and pleaded this question: "Do you know what it is to be really hungry? Do you know what it is to really be thirsty? Do you desire righteousness as you would desire food under extreme conditions or drink under extreme conditions? [The Savior] expects us to literally hunger and thirst after righteousness and seek it with all our hearts!"

I was one of the few present on that occasion who knew how hungry and thirsty Elder Petersen really was. His encroaching cancer had deprived him of relief from physical hunger and thirst. So he understood that doctrine. He withstood the trial. He thanked the Lord who lent him power to preach his last major sermon at the sacred site where his Lord Jesus had preached. ("I'll Go, I'll Do, I'll Be," B.Y.U. Education Week Devotional, August 19, 1986.)

The second caution is that we should not assume that the desires of our hearts, which can apparently serve as compliance with a *law* of the gospel, can also serve as compliance with an *ordinance* of the gospel.

There is no scriptural authority for the proposition that good intent can substitute for the performance of a required *ordinance*. Consider the words of the Lord in commanding two gospel ordinances. (1) "Verily, verily, I say unto thee," Jesus said, "Except a man be born of water and of the Spirit, he cannot enter into the kingdom of God" (John 3:5). The way to be "born of water" is to be "baptized," and the way to be "born of the Spirit" is to be "quickened in the inner man" by receiving the Holy Ghost

(Moses 6:65–66). (2) With reference to the three degrees in the celestial glory, modern revelation states, "In order to obtain the highest, a man must enter into this order of the priesthood [meaning the new and everlasting covenant of marriage]" (D&C 131:2). No exception is implied in these commands or authorized elsewhere in the scriptures.

Those scriptures that declare persons to be "heirs" of the celestial kingdom on the basis of their desires (D&C 137:7–8) are not contrary to this principle. In his vision of the world of departed spirits, President Joseph F. Smith saw faithful elders who had departed mortal life continue their labors preaching the gospel "among those who are in darkness and under the bondage of sin in the great world of the spirits of the dead" (D&C 138:57). He described the outcome of this preaching:

> The dead who repent will be redeemed, through obedience to the ordinances of the house of God,
>
> And after they have paid the penalty of their transgressions, and are washed clean, shall receive a reward according to their works, for they are heirs of salvation. (D&C 138:58–59.)

These spirits are "heirs of salvation," but it is still necessary for them to be redeemed "through obedience to the ordinances of the house of God" (D&C 138:58). In contrast, children who die before the age of accountability are not referred to in terms of heirship or in terms of required ordinances. Such children are, in the words of the Lord, "saved in the celestial kingdom of heaven" (D&C 137:10).

Ordinances are required, and there apparently are no exceptions based on the righteous desires of our hearts. But in the justice and mercy of God, the rigid effects of the commands pertaining to essential ordinances are tempered by divine authorization to perform those ordinances by proxy for those who did not have the opportunity to have

In the justice of God we will ultimately be judged and rewarded for what we are. And what we are is the sum total of our good and our evil actions and desires.

---

them performed in this life. A person in the spirit world who desires to accept the gospel can be credited with participating in the ordinances just as if he or she had done so personally. In this manner, through the loving service of living proxies, departed spirits are also rewarded for the desires of their hearts.

Our life is a time of trial and testing, just as the Lord tested Israel for forty years in the wilderness. The purpose of that testing, the Lord explained, was "to humble thee, and to prove thee, to know what was in thine heart, whether thou wouldest keep his commandments, or no" (Deuteronomy 8:2).

In the justice of God we will ultimately be judged and rewarded for what we are. And what we are is the sum total of our good and our evil actions and desires.

CHAPTER FIVE

MATERIALISM

The Book of Mormon tells of a time when the church of God "began to fail in its progress" because "the people of the church began to . . . set their hearts upon riches and upon the vain things of the world" (Alma 4:8, 10). Those who set their hearts upon the things of the world usually focus on some combination of that worldly quartet of property, pride, prominence, and power. When attitudes or priorities are fixed on the acquisition, use, or possession of property, we call that condition materialism. (Pride is discussed in the next chapter.)

In descending order of intensity, materialism may be an obsession, a preoccupation, or merely a strong interest. Whatever its degree, an interest becomes materialism when it is intense enough to override priorities that should be paramount.

From the emphasis given to this subject in the scriptures, it appears that materialism has been one of the greatest challenges to the children of God in all ages of time. Greed, the ugly face of materialism in action, has been one of Satan's most effective weapons in corrupting men and turning their hearts from God.

In the first of the Ten Commandments, accepted as fundamental religious law by Christians and Jews alike, God commands: "Thou shalt have no other gods before me" (Exodus 20:3). This is obviously much more than a prohibition against the overt worship of images like the god Baal. (Idol worship is the subject of the second commandment, "Thou shalt not make unto thee any graven image" [Exodus 20:4].) The first commandment is a comprehensive prohibition against the pursuit of any goal or priority ahead of God. The first commandment prohibits materialism.

The Savior and his Apostles gave many warnings against setting our hearts upon the treasures of this world.

Jesus taught that we should not lay up for ourselves "treasures upon earth, where moth and rust doth corrupt, and where thieves break through and steal: . . . For where your treasure is, there will your heart be also." (Matthew 6:19, 21.) In other words, the treasures of our hearts—our priorities—should not be the destructible and temporary things of this world.

In elaborating the parable of the sower, the Savior explained that the seed that fell "among the thorns" signified the circumstance of one who heard the message of the gospel, but "the care of this world, and the deceitfulness of riches, choke the word, and he becometh unfruitful" (Matthew 13:22). We have all seen examples of this pattern of stunted growth. After the precious seed (the message of the gospel) has begun to grow in the lives of some persons, they are diverted by their attention to the things of the world, and their spiritual fruits are choked out by "the deceitfulness of riches."

Those who preach the gospel of success and the theology of prosperity are suffering from "the deceitfulness of riches" and from supposing that "gain is godliness." The possession of wealth or the acquisition of significant income is not a mark of heavenly favor, and their absence is not evidence of heavenly disfavor.

The deceitfulness of riches can choke out the fruits of the gospel in many ways. A person who covets the wealth of another will suffer spiritually. A person who has wealth and then loses it and becomes embittered and hateful is also a victim of the deceitfulness of riches.

Another victim is the person who becomes resentful of the wealth of the wicked. The prophet Jeremiah gave voice to the old question, "Wherefore doth the way of the wicked prosper? wherefore are all they happy that deal very treacherously?" (Jeremiah 12:1.) Those who brood over the prosperity or seeming happiness of the wicked put too much emphasis on material things. They can be deceived because their priorities are too concentrated on worldly wealth.

Another victim of the deceitfulness of riches is the person who consciously or unconsciously feels guilt at having failed to acquire the property or prominence the world credits as the indicia of success.

Those who preach the gospel of success and the theology of prosperity are suffering from "the deceitfulness of riches" and from supposing that "gain is godliness" (1 Timothy 6:5). The possession of wealth or the acquisition of significant income is not a mark of heavenly favor, and their absence is not evidence of heavenly disfavor.

Riches can be among the blessings that follow right behavior—such as the payment of tithing (Malachi 3:9–12)—
but riches can also be acquired through the luck of a pros-
pector or as the fruits of dishonesty.

Elder Neal A. Maxwell reminds us that those who trust
in riches fail to see the real purpose of life:

> Jesus counseled us, too, concerning materialism and "the
> deceitfulness of riches" (Matthew 13:22), and of how hard it
> is for those who trust in riches and materialism to enter into
> the kingdom of God. (See Luke 18:24.) . . . Can those who
> are diverted by riches or the search for riches and thus fail to
> discern the real purposes of life be safely trusted with greater
> dominions which call for even greater discernment? "And he
> that overcometh, and keepeth my works unto the end, to him
> will I give power over the nations." (Revelation 2:26.)
> ("Thanks Be to God," *Ensign*, July 1982, p. 53.)

Another lesson on materialism is taught in the example
of the follower who asked the Savior what he should do to
"inherit eternal life." After this questioner represented
that he had kept all the commandments from his youth,
the Savior said: "One thing thou lackest: go thy way, sell
whatsoever thou hast, and give to the poor, and thou shalt
have treasure in heaven: and come, take up the cross, and
follow me." When the follower heard this, "he was sad at
that saying, and went away grieved: for he had great possessions." Seeing this, Jesus said, "How hard it is for
them that trust in riches to enter into the kingdom of
God!" (Mark 10:17, 21, 22, 24).

This man's failing was not his *possession* of riches but
his *attitude* toward them. As was demonstrated by his
apparent failure to follow the Savior's challenge, he still
lacked the attitude toward the things of this world that is
required to "inherit eternal life." As the Prophet Joseph
Smith taught in our own day, "A religion that does not
require the sacrifice of all things never has power sufficient

76

to produce the faith necessary unto life and salvation'' (*Lectures on Faith* 6:7).

In the midst of prophetic utterances about his Second Coming, the Savior warned that we should not be so preoccupied with the cares of this life that we are unprepared for that great day: ''And take heed to yourselves, lest at any time your hearts be overcharged with surfeiting, and drunkenness, and cares of this life, and so that day come upon you unawares'' (Luke 21:34).

The Savior taught the multitude to seek treasures in heaven rather than treasures on earth and cautioned them that they ''cannot serve God and Mammon'' (3 Nephi 13:24; Matthew 6:24). After teaching this general principle, he applied it specifically to the leaders he had called as full-time ministers. Jesus ''looked upon the twelve whom he had chosen'' and told them how far they must go in putting aside the priorities of the world:

> Remember the words which I have spoken. For behold, ye are they whom I have chosen to minister unto this people. Therefore I say unto you, take no thought for your life, what ye shall eat, or what ye shall drink; nor yet for your body, what ye shall put on. Is not the life more than meat, and the body than raiment? (3 Nephi 13:25; see also Matthew 6:25).

The New Testament has many other significant teachings on materialism.

''Set your affection on things above,'' the Apostle Paul wrote, ''not on things on the earth'' (Colossians 3:2). Paul was obviously no preacher or practitioner of the gospel of success or the theology of prosperity. ''For,'' as he told the Corinthian Saints, ''I determined not to know any thing among you, save Jesus Christ, and him crucified'' (1 Corinthians 2:2).

Paul cautioned young Timothy to withdraw from ''men of corrupt minds, and destitute of the truth, [who] sup-

> **Paul did not say that there was anything inherently evil about money. As we are all aware, the Good Samaritan used the same coinage to serve his fellowman and win the Savior's praise as Judas did to betray him. It is not money but the love of money that is identified as the root of all evil.**

pos[e] that gain is godliness'' (1 Timothy 6:5). Those who aspire to wealth should take further note of what he said next:

> They that will be rich fall into temptation and a snare, and into many foolish and hurtful lusts, which drown men in destruction and perdition.
>
> For the love of money is the root of all evil. (1 Timothy 6:9–10.)

The Apostle did not say that there was anything inherently evil about money. As we are all aware, the Good Samaritan used the same coinage to serve his fellowman and win the Savior's praise as Judas did to betray him. It is not money but the *love* of money that is identified as the root of all evil.

Paul instructed Timothy to teach this to those who have wealth:

> Charge them that are rich in this world, that they be not highminded, nor trust in uncertain riches, but in the living God, who giveth us richly all things to enjoy;
>
> That they do good, that they be rich in good works, ready to distribute, willing to communicate;
>
> Laying up in store for themselves a good foundation against the time to come, that they may lay hold on eternal life. (1 Timothy 6:17–19.)

The wise author of Proverbs warned against what we now call materialism: "Labour not to be rich: cease from thine own wisdom. Wilt thou set thine eyes upon that which is not? for riches certainly make themselves wings; they fly away as an eagle toward heaven." (Proverbs 23:4–5.)

The Book of Mormon identifies the love of riches and the pride it engenders as the cause of the spiritual and temporal downfall of the people of God.

When Lehi's descendants had established themselves successfully in the New World, Jacob cautioned them against the spiritual dangers of riches:

> But wo unto the rich, who are rich as to the things of the world. For because they are rich they despise the poor, and they persecute the meek, and their hearts are upon their treasures; wherefore, their treasure is their God. (2 Nephi 9:30.)

Later, Nephi warned how the devil would seek to thwart the work of God in the last days by leading the children of men astray. One of his methods will subvert us by means of property and prosperity:

> And others will he pacify, and lull them away into carnal security, that they will say: All is well in Zion; yea, Zion prospereth, all is well—and thus the devil cheateth their souls, and leadeth them away carefully down to hell (2 Nephi 28:21).

When we place our trust in our property, we have "carnal security." In that state of mind we are inclined to say that all must be well with us and with Zion *because* we are prospering, thus relying on worldly success as a mark of divine favor. He who does this is an easy mark for being led "carefully down to hell."

A wealthy man died. "How much property did he leave?" someone inquired. The wise response: "He left all of it."

The prophet Jacob taught the people that the acquisition of riches was not evil if it was done for the right reasons and in the right sequence:

> Before ye seek for riches, seek ye for the kingdom of God.
> And after ye have obtained a hope in Christ ye shall obtain riches, if ye seek them; and ye will seek them for the intent to do good—to clothe the naked, and to feed the hungry, and to liberate the captive, and administer relief to the sick and the afflicted. (Jacob 2:18–19.)

"Why do ye set your hearts upon riches?" the prophet Abinadi asked the wicked king and priests of his day (Mosiah 12:29).

The prophet Alma counseled one of his sons: "Seek not after riches nor the vain things of this world; for behold, you cannot carry them with you" (Alma 39:14).

A wealthy man died. "How much property did he leave?" someone inquired. The wise response: "He left all of it."

John Wesley, the Protestant reformer who founded Methodism, described this relationship between riches and religion:

> I fear, wherever riches have increased, the essence of religion has decreased in the same proportion. Therefore I do not see how it is possible, in the nature of things, for any revival of true religion to continue long. For religion must necessarily produce both industry and frugality, and these cannot but produce riches. But as riches increase so will pride, anger, and love of the world in all its branches. (Robert Southey, *The Life of Wesley; and the Rise and*

Progress of Methodism, vol. 2 [New York: Evert Duyckinck, 1820], p. 235.)

The prophet Mormon commented that Satan, "the author of all sin, . . . got great hold upon the hearts of the Nephites; yea, insomuch that they . . . did build up unto themselves idols of their gold and their silver" (Helaman 6:30–31).

The message of the modern prophets is the same as the ancient ones: If we set our hearts upon riches, we have set a worldly god ahead of the eternal God of Israel.

President Brigham Young feared that the Latter-day Saints would succumb to materialism. Less than two years after their arrival in the valley of the Great Salt Lake, he spoke these words to the people:

> The worst fear that I have about this people is that they will get rich in this country, forget God and His people, wax fat, and kick themselves out of the Church and go to hell. This people will stand mobbing, robbing, poverty, and all manner of persecution, and be true. But my greater fear for them is that they cannot stand wealth; and yet they have to be tried with riches, for they will become the richest people on this earth." (Reported in James S. Brown, *Life of a Pioneer,* pp. 122–23 [1900]; quoted in Bryant S. Hinckley, *The Faith of Our Pioneer Fathers* [Salt Lake City: Deseret Book Co., 1956], p. 13.)

Elder James E. Faust has taught:

> The relationship of money to happiness is at best questionable. Even the *Wall Street Journal* acknowledged, "Money is an article which may be used as a universal passport to everywhere except heaven, and as a universal provider of everything except happiness." Henrik Ibsen wrote, "Money may buy the husk of many things, but not the kernel. It brings you food, but not the appetite; medicine, but not health; acquaintances, but not friends; servants, but not faithfulness; days of joy, but not peace or happiness."

"The danger of all progress is idolatry, because the temptation all of the time is to set up something in the place of God. And the more tempting the progress is—and material prosperity is tempting—the more dangerous it is. Think of the idols of prosperity: the car, the camper, the boat, the color TV, the football game, two weeks of hunting. These become idols when more enthusiasm and time are given to them than to the worship of God."

(James E. Faust, *To Reach Even Unto You* [Salt Lake City: Deseret Book Co., 1980], p. 8.)

Americans are often criticized for materialism. Writing about the United States of the 1830s, a distinguished European observer, Alexis de Tocqueville, said he knew of no country "where the love of money has taken a stronger hold on the affections of men" (*Democracy in America*, 1835, part I, ch. 3). Many informed foreign observers still see the citizens of the United States as materialistic. Arthur Henry King, a distinguished British scholar and Latter-day Saint, shares this perspective:

American Mormons, and Americans generally, are threatened at a more fundamental level by the material prosperity of this country. It is a curse in disguise. Prosperity *per se* is not an enemy to religion, but prosperity may often lead to idolatry. The danger of all progress is idolatry, because the temptation all of the time is to set up something in the place of God. And the more tempting the progress is—and material prosperity is tempting—the more dangerous it is. Think of the idols of prosperity: the car, the camper, the boat (bane of bishops), the color TV, the football game, two weeks of hunting. These become idols when more enthusiasm and time are given to them than to the worship of God. (*The*

Abundance of the Heart [Salt Lake City: Bookcraft, 1986], p. 48.)

A modern prophet, President Spencer W. Kimball, expressed this concern for the materialism of many modern Latter-day Saints:

Many people spend most of their time working in the service of a self-image that includes sufficient money, stocks, bonds, investment portfolios, property, credit cards, furnishings, automobiles, and the like to *guarantee* carnal security throughout, it is hoped, a long and happy life. Forgotten is the fact that our assignment is to use these many resources in our families and quorums to build up the kingdom of God— to further the missionary effort and the genealogical and temple work; to raise our children up as fruitful servants unto the Lord; to bless others in every way, that they may also be fruitful. Instead, we expend these blessings on our own desires.

President Kimball explained why he called this attitude "idolatry":

Carnal man has tended to transfer his trust in God to material things. . . . Whatever thing a man sets his heart and his trust in most is his god; and if his god doesn't also happen to be the true and living God of Israel, that man is laboring in idolatry. ("The False Gods We Worship," *Ensign*, June 1976, pp. 4–5.)

Some have charged that modern Latter-day Saints are peculiarly susceptible to the gospel of success and the theology of prosperity. According to this gospel, success in this world—particularly entrepreneurial success—is an essential ingredient of progress toward the celestial kingdom. According to this theology, success and prosperity are rewards for keeping the commandments, and a large home and an expensive car are marks of heavenly favor. Those who make this charge point to the apparent susceptibility of Utahns (predominantly Latter-day Saints) to the speculative proposals of various get-rich-quick artists. They claim that many Utahns are gullible and overeager for wealth.

Certainly, Utah has had many victims of speculative enterprises. For at least a decade there have been a succession of frauds worked by predominantly Mormon entrepreneurs upon predominantly Mormon victims. Stock manipulations; residential mortgage financings; gold, silver, diamonds, uranium, and document investments; pyramid schemes—all have taken their toll upon the faithful and gullible. Whether inherently too trusting or just naively overeager for a shortcut to the material prosperity some see as the badge of righteousness, some Latter-day Saints are apparently too vulnerable to the lure of sudden wealth.

Objective observers differ on whether Latter-day Saints are *more* susceptible to get-rich-quick proposals than other citizens. However that may be, it is disturbing that there is no clear evidence that Latter-day Saints are *less* susceptible. Men and women who have heard and taken to heart the scriptural warnings against materialism should not be vulnerable to the deceitfulness of riches and the extravagant blandishments of its promoters.

The unscrupulous Christians who have aggressively promoted the priorities of materialism and preyed upon the victims of that philosophy come within the prophet Isaiah's condemnation of the sinner who benefits by "the gain of oppressions":

> The sinners in Zion are afraid; fearfulness hath surprised the hypocrites. Who among us shall dwell with the devouring fire? who among us shall dwell with everlasting burnings?
>
> He that walketh righteously, and speaketh uprightly; he that despiseth the gain of oppressions. (Isaiah 33:14–15.)

Materialism is a seductive distortion of self-reliance. The corruption occurs through carrying the virtue of "providing for our own" to the point of excess concern with accumulating the treasures of the earth.

In order to "dwell with everlasting burnings"—an obvious reference to the celestial kingdom—we must "despise the gain of oppressions." We must also be so indifferent to material or earthly things that we are willing to give up cheerfully whatever is necessary to become "equal" in those things (D&C 70:14; 78:5–6). We must be tested by this divinely revealed standard of behavior, which is the polar opposite of aggressive and selfish materialism: "Every man seeking the interest of his neighbor, and doing all things with an eye single to the glory of God" (D&C 82:19).

If Latter-day Saints are specially susceptible to materialism, this may be because materialism is a corruption of a virtue in which Latter-day Saints take special pride. Materialism is a seductive distortion of self-reliance. The corruption occurs through carrying the virtue of "providing for our own" to the point of excess concern with accumulating the treasures of the earth.

Most Latter-day Saints have some acquaintances who seem preoccupied with acquiring and possessing worldly goods. Their sense of personal worth seems to be measured by their "net worth." Persons in this circumstance are vulnerable to spiritual as well as economic depressions. As Stephen R. Covey has observed, "When a person's sense of personal worth comes from his net worth, when it is the ground of his being, then he is totally vulnerable to anything that will affect that net worth" (*The Divine Center* [Salt Lake City: Bookcraft, 1982], p. 29).

"I come to see that the things which men give in the way of honor and respect and office and position are really of little worth. They are not worth what sometimes we feel we have to give in order to obtain them. I come to know that worldly goods are of no consequence whatever, save I have enough to eat, and to drink and reasonably to wear."

One person with an especially intense preoccupation with material things was the object of an unfulfilled conspiracy by two LDS friends. They quietly plotted to present him with a framed stitchery containing a slogan that seemed appropriate for him: "Inner peace through materialism."

During the past half-century many Americans, including many Latter-day Saints, have been vigorously and successfully involved in defending our way of life against communism. Perhaps a preoccupation with turning communism away from the front door has made us vulnerable to the corruption of materialism slipping in through the back door. Communism is evil because it deprives people of their freedom and teaches that there is no God. Materialism is evil because it corrupts people in the use of their freedom and substitutes the god of property for the God of heaven.

Toward the end of his life, President J. Reuben Clark shared his reflections about "the things which are of lasting importance." Though he had received many honors and was possessed of the power, prominence, and professional qualifications that could have been used to accumulate much wealth, President Clark concluded that worldly things were of no consequence:

I come to see that the things which men give in the way of honor and respect and office and position are really of little worth. They are not worth what sometimes we feel we have to give in order to obtain them. I come to know that worldly goods are of no consequence whatever, save I have enough to eat, and to drink and reasonably to wear, and that to attempt to leave wealth to my children will not only be a futile effort but that it may prove a curse.

I do not mean by this that we should cease to exert our efforts to become influential for good in our communities. I do not mean that we should forget that we are living here and have our lives to live. I do not forget that a reasonable provision for those who come after us is a wise thing. I am only saying that none of these things is worth the sacrifice of a principle. They are not worth the sacrifice of our integrity, of our honor, of our righteous living. (Conference Report, October 1948, p. 78.)

Like President Clark, most Latter-day Saints do not succumb to materialism. There is ample evidence that they adhere to eternal values to a greater extent than any other people. They make the financial sacrifices necessary to "be fruitful, and multiply, and replenish the earth" (Moses 2:28) by large families. They pay tithing. They serve missions at their own expense. They cheerfully donate their professional skills in service to their church and their fellowmen. They accept and fulfill the responsibilities of Church callings. To an impressive extent, Latter-day Saints obey God's command: "Thou shalt have no other gods before me" (Exodus 20:3).

CHAPTER SIX

PRIDE

Pride is a word of many meanings. This chapter will discuss three meanings that involve gospel values.

The Appropriate Pride of Self-Respect

In terms of gospel values, some manifestations of pride are acceptable. There is a kind of pride that is akin to self-respect. It comes from measuring ourselves against an objective standard. There is nothing wrong with a workman who takes "pride" in his work. As Elder Marvin J. Ashton has observed, "Appropriate personal pride prohibits shabby performance" (*What Is Your Destination?* [Salt Lake City: Deseret Book Co., 1978], p. 105).

The commendable performance of a difficult task is a proper source of pride. Elder Stephen L Richards declared:

That pride in a man which makes him cherish his own good name and gives him the courage to work to sustain it, that pride which makes him shun the bondage of undischargeable obligations, that pride which keeps his head high even in poverty, conscious that he has always been honorable, and has given the best that was in him, that pride I admire. I think, too, it is essential for the preservation of some of the best things within our civilization. Self-respect, self-reliance, and the pride of achievement I look upon as highly prominent factors in our economic welfare, and in our spiritual as well. (*Where Is Wisdom?* [Salt Lake City: Deseret Book Co., 1955], p. 412.)

That kind of pride builds people and communities.

The Scriptures Condemn Pride

Other kinds of pride are condemned in the scriptures. In his keynote address at the general conference where he was sustained as President of the Church, President Ezra Taft Benson declared: "In the scriptures there is no such thing as righteous pride. It is always considered as a sin." ("Cleansing the Inner Vessel," *Ensign*, May 1986, p. 6.)

The scriptures abound with condemnations and cautions about pride. "Be not proud," the prophet Jeremiah proclaimed (Jeremiah 13:15). The author of Proverbs declares that "pride goeth before destruction, and an haughty spirit before a fall" (Proverbs 16:18).

Many scriptures declare that in the last day all they that "do wickedly" and all the "proud" shall be burned as "stubble" (Malachi 4:1; 1 Nephi 22:15; 3 Nephi 25:1; D&C 29:9; 64:24; 133:64). It is significant that this important prophecy includes both those who *do* wickedly and those who *think* wickedly (pride).

Similarly, Proverbs states: "Everyone that is proud in heart is an abomination to the Lord: though hand join in

A person who has the pride of self-satisfaction cannot repent, because he recognizes no shortcomings. This kind of pride has a self-image that has inflated from wholesome positive to excessive preoccupied. In contrast to the spiritual wholeness of the self-forgetful, this kind of pride bespeaks the spiritual extremity of the self-centered.

---

hand, he shall not be unpunished" (Proverbs 16:5). "Hand join in hand" is probably a reference to good actions, perhaps typified by the one who extends a hand to help those in need. It is noteworthy that even though a person has engaged in such good actions, if he is "proud in heart" he is still an "abomination" and "shall not be unpunished." The Savior taught that pride was one of the things that comes from "within" that "defile the man" (Mark 7:22–23).

The remainder of this chapter will discuss two kinds of pride that are condemned in the scriptures, and will then examine how their evil effects are illustrated in the Book of Mormon.

The Pride of Self-Satisfaction

One kind of pride condemned in the scriptures is synonymous with self-satisfaction. The pride of self-satisfaction is self-righteous. Self-righteousness is "a condition of soul that assumes and creates an air-tight justification for everything you do simply because you do it" (Norman Podhoretz, "Candidates' Morality Is Not Private," *Insight*, June 8, 1987, p. 64).

But what I call the pride of self-satisfaction goes deeper than mere self-justification. Self-satisfaction is the opposite of humility. A person who has the pride of self-satisfaction cannot repent, because he recognizes no shortcomings. He cannot be taught, because he recognizes no master. He cannot be helped, because he recognizes no resource greater than his own. This kind of pride has a self-image that has inflated from wholesome positive to excessive preoccupied. In contrast to the spiritual wholeness of the self-forgetful, this kind of pride bespeaks the spiritual extremity of the self-centered.

Preoccupied with self, the pride of self-satisfaction is always accompanied by an aloofness and a withdrawal from concern for others. Henry Fairlie wrote of this kind of pride:

> Pride may excite us to take too much pleasure in ourselves, but it does not encourage us to take pleasure in our humanity, in what is commonly shared by all of us as social beings. The turning into ourselves has turned us away from our societies. It is a sin of neglect: it causes us to ignore others. It is a sin of aggression: it provokes us to hurt others. It is a sin of condescension: it makes us patronize others. All of these are turned against our neighbors, and often in our Pride we do not realize how aloof we have become, and how cut off even from what in our own nature we should most deeply know and enjoy.

Fairlie concludes that our self-absorption has produced a "self-improvement" that "is measured only by how good one feels about oneself." In this there is only "discontent," which "is always one of the punishments of Pride, the consequence of the illusions of self-sufficiency that it encourages." (Henry Fairlie, *The Seven Deadly Sins Today* [Washington, D.C.: New Republic Books, 1978], pp. 45, 52.)

The pride of self-satisfaction is the pride Alma meant when he told his son Shiblon: "See that ye are not lifted up unto pride; yea, see that ye do not boast in your own wisdom, nor of your much strength'' (Alma 38:11). The consequences of the pride of self-satisfaction in Helaman's time are described in these words:

> And because of this their great wickedness, and their boastings in their own strength, they were left in their own strength; therefore they did not prosper, but were afflicted and smitten, and driven before the Lamanites, until they had lost possession of almost all their lands (Helaman 4:13).

The pride of self-satisfaction is probably the kind of pride that prominent members were warned against in the early revelations of this dispensation (D&C 23:1 [Oliver Cowdery]; 25:14 [Emma Smith]; 56:8 [Ezra Thayre]). In a sermon delivered in Nauvoo, Illinois, the Prophet Joseph Smith said: ''There are a great many wise men and women too in our midst who are too wise to be taught; therefore they must die in their ignorance, and in the resurrection they will find their mistake'' (*History of the Church* 5:424).

We still have a great many ''wise men and women too in our midst who are too wise to be taught.'' And no one suffers more from their condition than they themselves.

Elder B. H. Roberts called this kind of pride ''intellectual pride; the pride of knowledge, . . . which so often attends upon the worldly learned men.'' He added:

> For my own part I can think of nothing that could be a greater offense against the majesty of God than for a man with his limited intellectual power presuming to pass judgment upon and rejecting the things of God, because forsooth, these things do not conform to his opinion of what the things of God should be like; or because the way in which they are revealed does not conform to the manner in which he thinks God should impart his truths. Such pride always has and always will separate men from receiving knowledge by divine communication.

As Alma taught, "he that will harden his heart, the same receiveth the lesser portion of the word" (Alma 12:10). In contrast, Elder Roberts noted:

> The meek and humble of spirit, borne down with a sense of their own limitations, find grace and spiritual enlightenment and comfort in the things which God reveals; and often arrive at hidden treasures of knowledge, and even of wisdom, unknown to the intellectually proud whom God resisteth. (*Liahona, The Elders Journal*, February 28, 1911, p. 580.)

In the words of Alma, "and he that will not harden his heart, to him is given the greater portion of the word, until it is given unto him to know the mysteries of God until he know them in full" (Alma 12:10).

The pride of self-satisfaction is extraordinarily difficult to overcome. As President Spencer W. Kimball wrote: "When one becomes conscious of his great humility, he has already lost it. When one begins boasting of his humility, it has already become pride—the antithesis of humility." (*The Teachings of Spencer W. Kimball* [Salt Lake City: Bookcraft, 1982], p. 233.)

Benjamin Franklin said that pride "is the last vice the good man gets clear of" (*Poor Richard's Almanac* 1732–57). In his autobiography he elaborated that thought:

> In reality, there is, perhaps, no one of our natural passions so hard to subdue as *pride*. Disguise it, struggle with it, beat it down, stifle it, mortify it as much as one pleases, it is still alive, and will every now and then peep out and show itself; you will see it, perhaps, often in this history; for, even if I could conceive that I had compleatly overcome it, I should probably be proud of my humility. (*The Autobiography of Benjamin Franklin*, Harvard Classics, vol. 1 [1909], p. 92.)

The pride of comparison is not just a high opinion of one's own qualities or attainments, or the "inordinate self-esteem" described in the dictionary. It is an attitude that commences with personal comparisons with others and leads to demeaning thoughts or oppressive actions directed at other sons and daughters of God.

The Pride of Comparison

The second type of pride that is condemned in the scriptures is what I have chosen to call the pride of comparison. Like the appropriate pride of self-respect, it follows on our concluding that we have done well in competition. But unlike the pride of self-respect, the competition is not with some outside *standard*, like a four-minute mile or an errorless performance of a difficult task. The pride of comparison is the mental attitude that comes from competing with *persons* and concluding that we are "better" than they. This is the kind of pride Elder L. Tom Perry condemned: "Those who are more prosperous can become filled with pride, and they look down on their brothers and sisters who have less, thinking them inferior" ("United in Building the Kingdom of God," *Ensign*, May 1987, p. 33).

Materialism is an attitude toward *things*. In contrast, the pride of comparison is an attitude toward *people*.

The pride of comparison may grow out of comparing riches, homes, cars, position, degrees, or other attainments, appearance, talent, wisdom, or any other natural or acquired attribute or possession.

This kind of pride is not just a high opinion of one's own qualities or attainments, or the "inordinate self-esteem"

"Pride does not look up to God and care about what is right. It looks sideways to man and argues who is right. Pride is manifest in the spirit of contention."

described in the dictionary. It is an attitude that commences with personal comparisons with others and leads to demeaning thoughts or oppressive actions directed at other sons and daughters of God.

The pride of self-satisfaction imposes its primary effects upon the one who is proud. His attitude blocks his own progress. In contrast, the pride of comparison is pernicious because of its tendency to the oppression of others.

C. S. Lewis described the pride of comparison when he said:

> Pride is *essentially* competitive. . . . Pride gets no pleasure out of having something, only out of having more of it than the next man. . . . It is the comparison that makes you proud: the pleasure of being above the rest.

Lewis called pride "the utmost evil" and "the complete anti-God state of mind," because this kind of comparison leads men to enmity and oppression and every other kind of evil. This insightful Christian saw that every person should look up to God as "immeasurably superior" to him or her. He continued:

> Unless you know God as that—and, therefore, know yourself as nothing in comparison—you do not know God at all. As long as you are proud you cannot know God. A proud man is always looking down on things and people: and, of course, as long as you are looking down, you cannot see something that is above you. (*Mere Christianity* [New York: Macmillan Publishing Co., Inc., 1960], pp. 109–11.)

President Ezra Taft Benson expressed a similar thought when he said:

Pride does not look up to God and care about what is right. It looks sideways to man and argues who is right. Pride is manifest in the spirit of contention. ("Cleansing the Inner Vessel," *Ensign*, May 1986, p. 6.)

As the author of Proverbs observed, "Only by pride cometh contention" (Proverbs 13:10), and "He that is of a proud heart stirreth up strife" (Proverbs 28:25).

The Book of Mormon contains our most extensive and illuminating teachings on the nature and effects of the pride of comparison.

When the Lord showed him the thoughts of the people, the prophet Jacob told them that he "must testify unto [them] concerning the wickedness of [their] hearts" (Jacob 2:6). After reminding them how they had been blessed to obtain riches, Jacob condemned the effect of their riches on their thoughts and their behavior:

> And because some of you have obtained more abundantly than that of your brethren ye are lifted up in the pride of your hearts, and wear stiff necks and high heads because of the costliness of your apparel, and persecute your brethren because ye suppose that ye are better than they (Jacob 2:13).

In this passage Jacob defined the elements of the pride of comparison: (1) a person obtains something more abundantly than others; (2) he is lifted up in pride because of this possession; and (3) he persecutes others because he supposes he is better than they. Jacob underlined the seriousness of this kind of pride when he pleaded, "Let not this pride of your hearts destroy your souls!" (Jacob 2:16).

In the Book of Mormon accounts, the pride of comparison resulted most frequently from the acquisition and use of riches, such as by wearing fine apparel. Thus, Alma the Younger gave this description of the Nephites in the land of Zarahemla, who "began to wax proud" because of their possessions, including their flocks, their gold, and their fine apparel: "The people of the church began to be lifted up in the pride of their eyes, and to set their hearts upon riches and upon the vain things of the world, that they began to be scornful, one towards another" (Alma 4:8).

As a result of this attitude of the people, there were "great contentions among the people of the church" (Alma 4:9). Alma saw "great inequality among the people, some lifting themselves up with their pride, despising others, turning their backs upon the needy" (Alma 4:12). "And the wickedness of the church was a great stumbling-block to those who did not belong to the church; and thus the church began to fail in its progress" (Alma 4:10).

In a modern revelation referring to riches, the Lord warned his Saints to "beware of pride, lest ye become as the Nephites of old" (D&C 38:39).

These scriptures have been the text for many sermons by modern prophets. Elder Orson Pratt used them to give this warning:

> But there is danger . . . if we become lifted up in the pride of our hearts and think, because we have gathered an abundance of the wealth of this world, that we are a little better than our poor brother who labors eight or ten hours a day at the hardest kind of labor. Any person having the name of Latter-day Saint who feels that he is better than, and distinguishes himself from, the poor and supposes that he belongs to a little higher class than they, is in danger. (*Journal of Discourses* 17:31.)

This was a favorite subject of Elder George Q. Cannon. In 1872 he told an audience in the Tabernacle:

> I should deplore the increase of wealth in our midst if it created class distinctions, if it should create a feeling that, "I am better than thou, because I wear a finer coat, dwell in a better house, ride in a finer carriage and have finer horses, or because my children are better schooled and better dressed than yours."

98

"Let us be more concerned about the adornment of our minds that are eternal, rather than adornment of our persons with things that are of no lasting benefit. Let us keep the commandments of God; let us live humble, and sweet, and pure. Let us not be lifted up in the pride of our hearts if we have been more successful than our neighbor financially, but let us evidence by loving kindness to every child of our Heavenly Father that we are grateful."

There is no sin in industry or in fine houses or fine farms or attractive apparel, he explained. But there is sin in being "lifted up in pride because God has bestowed them upon us," and in thinking we are better than others:

> But this is the great difficulty and has been from the beginning. When wealth multiplies, the people get lifted up in pride of their hearts, and they look down on their poor brethren and despise them, because they are better educated, have better manners, and speak better language—in a word, because they have advantages which their poor brethren and sisters have not. There is sin in this, and God is angry with a people who take this course. (*Journal of Discourses* 15:156.)

In 1880 President George Q. Cannon read to an audience chapter 4 of Alma (quoted above), and then cautioned them against the love of riches, forgetting God as the source of our prosperity, and classifications in society based on wealth, dress, or housing. As to the latter, he said:

> Distinctions of this kind grew up not out of the Gospel, but out of the violation of the principles of the Gospel. Wherever the Gospel of the Lord Jesus Christ is taught, it produces, as I have said, this sense of equality, it makes the man who may know and understand the things of God feel that he is no

better than his fellow man, and the woman who understands the things of God feel that she is no better than her sister. (*Journal of Discourses* 22:100.)

In the same vein, Elder George Albert Smith spoke these words to a general conference audience in 1915:

> Let us be more concerned about the adornment of our minds that are eternal, rather than adornment of our persons with things that are of no lasting benefit. Let us keep the commandments of God; let us live humble, and sweet, and pure. Let us not be lifted up in the pride of our hearts if we have been more successful than our neighbor financially, but, mindful of the blessings of health and strength, and the gift of home and loved ones, appreciating the knowledge of the Gospel of Jesus Christ. . . . Let us evidence by loving kindness to every child of our Heavenly Father that we are grateful. (Conference Report, April 1915, pp. 97–98.)

Two of the Savior's parables illustrate and condemn the pride that comes from comparing ourselves with other men. The first of these was spoken "unto certain which trusted in themselves that they were righteous, and despised others" (Luke 18:9):

> Two men went up into the temple to pray; the one a Pharisee, and the other a publican.
> The Pharisee stood and prayed thus with himself, God, I thank thee, that I am not as other men are, extortioners, unjust, adulterers, or even as this publican.
> I fast twice in the week, I give tithes of all that I possess.
> And the publican, standing afar off, would not lift up so much as his eyes unto heaven, but smote upon his breast, saying, God be merciful to me a sinner. (Luke 18:10–13.)

We should note that the Pharisee was proud because he compared himself with other men. In so doing, he exalted himself above others. In contrast, the publican measured himself against the commandments of God, saw his abased

"No man can compare himself with his ideals and be proud or haughty. The proud and the haughty are only they who compare themselves with more unfortunate people than they."

---

and sinful state, and cried out for mercy. The Savior concluded the parable with this teaching about the publican:

> I tell you, this man went down to his house justified rather than the other: for every one that exalteth himself shall be abased; and he that humbleth himself shall be exalted (Luke 18:14).

This same teaching followed the second parable. There the Savior described how his followers should conduct themselves to avoid shame when they were invited to the home of the Master:

> When thou art bidden of any man to a wedding, sit not down in the highest room; lest a more honourable man than thou be bidden of him;
> And he that bade thee and him come and say to thee, Give this man place; and thou begin with shame to take the lowest room.
> But when thou art bidden, go and sit down in the lowest room; that when he that bade thee cometh, he may say unto thee, Friend, go up higher: then shalt thou have worship in the presence of them that sit at meat with thee. (Luke 14:8–10.)

In this way the Savior used a current circumstance to teach an eternal principle about attitudes toward others and ourselves. The proud man, who goes to a wedding and compares himself to the other guests, may conclude that he is better than they and seat himself in the highest room. The humble man, who has great reverence and respect for his host and who thinks only of his good fortune to be invited at all, will seat himself in the lowest room. Out of these contrasting attitudes—one pridefully comparing himself to other men and the other humbly appreciating his inadequacy in the house of his Master—came the Savior's conclusion:

> For whosoever exalteth himself shall be abased; and he that humbleth himself shall be exalted (Luke 14:11).

As Elder Antoine R. Ivins said: "No man can compare himself with his ideals and be proud or haughty. The proud and the haughty are only they who compare themselves with more unfortunate people than they." (Conference Report, October 1943, p. 110.)

Differences in money are not the only nesting ground for pride. Differences in talents or accomplishments or positions can also provide occasion for the destructive pride of comparison. In a sermon delivered to members of the Twelve as they were about to leave on their mission to Great Britain in 1839, the Prophet Joseph Smith gave this warning:

> Let the Twelve be humble, and not be exalted, and beware of pride, and not seek to excel one above another, but act for each other's good, and pray for one another, and honor our brother or make honorable mention of his name, and not backbite and devour our brother.

The Prophet gave this specific illustration:

> When the Twelve or any other witnesses stand before the congregations of the earth, and they preach in the power and demonstration of the Spirit of God, and the people are astonished and confounded at the doctrine, and say, "That man has preached a powerful discourse, a great sermon," then let that man or those men take care that they do not ascribe the glory unto themselves, but be careful that they are humble, and ascribe the praise and glory to God and the Lamb; for it is by the power of the Holy Priesthood and the Holy Ghost

Pride must be a special challenge in this dispensation, because the Book of Mormon, which was written to the people of our day, contains the most intensive and repetitive teachings about the evils of pride. It identifies pride as the cause of the spiritual and temporal downfall of the people of God.

---

that they have power thus to speak (*Teachings of the Prophet Joseph Smith*, sel. Joseph Fielding Smith [Salt Lake City: Deseret Book Co., 1938], pp. 155–56).

The Twelve remembered this counsel, and shared it with the Saints in Great Britain:

And now let the Saints remember that which we have ever taught them, both by precept and example, viz: to beware of an aspiring spirit, which would lift you up one above another: to seek to be the *greatest* in the kingdom of God. (Epistle of the Twelve, *Millennial Star*, May 1841, 1:310.)

Men become "puffed up in the pride of their hearts" from wisdom and learning as well as from riches (2 Nephi 28:15).

There is ample scriptural support for these warnings that leaders and members not succumb to pride in the course of their strivings in the kingdom. Pride is a jeopardy for the righteous as well as the wicked. It is one way the adversary can fix on a person's strengths (such as superior accomplishments or qualifications) and use them to cause his spiritual downfall.

In calling them as the initial First Presidency of this dispensation, the Lord admonished Joseph Smith, Sidney Rigdon, and Frederick G. Williams about their "high-mindedness and pride, for it bringeth a snare upon your souls" (D&C 90:17). Included among the ways that a holder of the priesthood can lose his authority is for him to attempt to use that authority "to gratify [his] pride" (D&C 121:37) rather than to accomplish the mission of the Master. This would include the use of priesthood authority to raise himself above others in ways not related to the position or activities of his priesthood calling, such as to obtain preferment in matters political or economic.

The Book of Mormon Chronicles the Effects of Pride

Pride must be a special challenge in this dispensation, because the Book of Mormon, which was written to the people of our day, contains the most intensive and repetitive teachings about the evils of pride. It identifies pride as the cause of the spiritual and temporal downfall of the people of God.

On the pride of self-satisfaction, the teachings of the prophets Alma and Helaman were discussed earlier. Nephi prophesied about this kind of pride in our own day:

> And the Gentiles are lifted up in the pride of their eyes, and have stumbled, because . . . they put down the power and miracles of God, and preach up unto themselves their own wisdom and their own learning, that they may get gain and grind upon the face of the poor (2 Nephi 26:20).

Most of the Book of Mormon teachings on pride concern the pride of comparison. The teachings of the prophets Jacob and Alma the Younger on that subject have already been quoted.

The most intensive applications of teachings on the pride of comparison occur in the period from about 130 B.C. to about A.D. 35. About three-fifths of the content of the Book of Mormon is concerned with this period of approximately 165 years. In that relatively brief period, equivalent to the time since the First Vision ushered in this final dispensation, the Book of Mormon records numerous cycles of righteousness and depravity. In every instance the prophets warned the people that a principal cause of their current or impending tragedy was the pride of their hearts, usually stemming from their love of riches.

After Alma the Younger gave the teachings on pride that were quoted earlier in this chapter, he relinquished his position as chief judge and (still being high priest) went forth to preach.

Alma told the people that if they were not "stripped of pride" they were "not prepared to meet God" or to have "eternal life" (Alma 5:28). He condemned those who were "puffed up" in the "vain things of the world" and "in the pride of [their] hearts" (Alma 5:37, 53). He asked: "Will ye still persist in the wearing of costly apparel and setting your hearts upon the vain things of the world . . . ? Yea, will ye persist in supposing that ye are better one than another; Yea, will ye persist in the persecution of your brethren?" (Alma 5:53–54). The pride of comparison seems to have a strong tendency toward persecution.

In his mission to the Zoramites, ten years later, Alma was grieved to see that their "hearts were set upon gold, and upon silver, and upon all manner of fine goods" and that their "hearts were lifted up unto great boasting, in their pride" (Alma 31:24–25).

Similarly, the people would not give heed to the words of Alma's son Helaman because they were "proud, being lifted up in their hearts, because of their exceedingly great riches" (Alma 45:24). A generation later, Helaman, the son of Helaman, found that "because of their exceedingly great riches and their prosperity in the land" pride had entered into the hearts of the people who "professed to belong to the church of God—and they were lifted up in pride, even to the persecution of many of their brethren" (Helaman 3:36, 33–34).

In the succeeding period the cycles were accelerated, and the civilization founded by the descendants of Lehi alternated between righteousness and degradation in astonishingly short periods of time.

Just a few years after Helaman's warning, the Nephites were so wicked that the righteous Lamanites sought to reclaim them (see Helaman 6:1–14). After a brief season of righteousness and happiness, the blessings of prosperity triggered their downfall. "They began to set their hearts upon their riches; yea, they began to seek to get gain that they might be lifted up one above another" (Helaman 6:17). A few years later, Nephi, the son of Helaman, told the Nephite people how they had brought themselves to forget God. He also prophesied the consequences:

> Behold, it is to get gain, to be praised of men, yea, and that ye might get gold and silver. And ye have set your hearts upon the riches and the vain things of this world. . . .
>
> Yea, wo shall come unto you because of that pride which ye have suffered to enter your hearts, which has lifted you up beyond that which is good because of your exceedingly great riches! (Helaman 7:21, 26.)

A few years later, many of the Nephites repented when their hearts were turned to the Lord by a famine (see Helaman 11). But prosperity soon brought more pride and wickedness. The prophet Nephi denounced them for their "unsteadiness" of heart. At the very time when the Lord had prospered his people, they "do harden their hearts" and forget the Lord "because of their ease, and their exceedingly great prosperity" (Helaman 12:1–2). Nephi sorrowed over how quickly the people "set their hearts upon the vain things of the world! Yea, how quick [they were] to be lifted up in pride." (Helaman 12:4–5.)

The Nephites of Zarahemla received this same message a year or so later from the Lamanite prophet, Samuel:

Ye do always remember your riches, not to thank the Lord your God for them; yea, your hearts are not drawn out unto the Lord, but they do swell with great pride, unto boasting, and unto great swelling, envyings, strifes, malice, persecutions, and murders, and all manner of iniquities'' (Helaman 13:22).

After being harassed by a band of robbers from about the year 13 until the year 22, the Nephites became faithful and diligent, and were blessed of the Lord (see 3 Nephi 5:1–3). Then they began to prosper, and by the year 29 ''some were lifted up unto pride and boastings because of their exceedingly great riches'' (3 Nephi 6:10).

And the people began to be distinguished by ranks, according to their riches and their chances for learning; yea, some were ignorant because of their poverty, and others did receive great learning because of their riches. . . .
And thus there became a great inequality in all the land, insomuch that the church began to be broken up. (3 Nephi 6:12–14.)

And so, the people again fell into iniquity. The prophet Nephi recorded the cause:

Now the cause of this iniquity of the people was this— Satan had great power, unto the stirring up of the people to do all manner of iniquity, and to the puffing them up with pride, tempting them to seek for power, and authority, and riches, and the vain things of the world.
And thus Satan did lead away the hearts of the people to do all manner of iniquity. (3 Nephi 6:15–16.)

By the year 30 they were ''in a state of awful wickedness'' in which ''they did wilfully rebel against God'' (3 Nephi 6:17, 18). Despite this, the prophet Nephi continued to preach and work mighty miracles, and a few of the people repented and were baptized (see 3 Nephi 7:21). Nephi's diligence was rewarded with "many" baptisms in the commencement of the year 33 (see 3 Nephi 7:23, 26).

Next came the destruction of the wicked at the time of the crucifixion of Christ (3 Nephi 8). The Savior appeared to the righteous survivors and ushered in a period of happiness that was to last more than 160 years. The righteous conditions of the people are described as follows:

> The people were all converted unto the Lord . . . and there were no contentions and disputations among them, and every man did deal justly one with another.
>
> And they had all things common among them; therefore there were not rich and poor, bond and free, but they were all made free, and partakers of the heavenly gift. (4 Nephi 1:2–3.)

During this great period of happiness, there would have been no basis for the pride of comparison, since "they had all [material] things common among them" (4 Nephi 1:3).

After about 160 years, "there began to be among them those who were lifted up in pride, such as the wearing of costly apparel. . . . And from that time forth they did have their goods and their substance no more common among them. And they began to be divided into classes." (4 Nephi 1:24–26.) These people "did harden their hearts" against the prophets (4 Nephi 1:31, 34), and "began to be proud in their hearts, because of their exceeding riches" (4 Nephi 1:43).

The descendants of Lehi never recovered from this downward cycle. After a hundred years "both the people of Nephi and the Lamanites had become exceedingly wicked one like unto another" (4 Nephi 1:45). The prophet Mormon was forbidden to preach to this people "because of the hardness of their hearts," and "the land was cursed for their sake" (Mormon 1:17). Mormon told his son Moroni, "the pride of . . . the people of the

**The pride of self-satisfaction is the opposite of
humility. This attitude insulates us from learning and
separates us from God. The pride of comparison is an
attitude of superiority toward other people as a result
of comparing our possessions, position, or attributes
with theirs. The pride of comparison is the opposite of
love.**

Nephites, hath proven their destruction except they should
repent" (Moroni 8:27).

Moroni, the son of Mormon and the last prophet of the
Book of Mormon, related the experiences of his people to
the prophesied conditions of our own day. He declared
that the Book of Mormon would come forth in a day when
"the power of God shall be denied," and when churches
and their leaders and teachers shall be "lifted up in the
pride of their hearts" (Mormon 8:28). Speaking to these,
the people of our day, he said:

> And I know that ye do walk in the pride of your hearts;
> and there are none save a few only who do not lift themselves
> up in the pride of their hearts, unto the wearing of very fine
> apparel, unto envying, and strifes, and malice, and persecu-
> tions, and all manner of iniquities. . . .
>
> For behold, ye do love money, and your substance, and
> your fine apparel, and the adorning of your churches, more
> than ye love the poor and the needy, the sick and the af-
> flicted. (Mormon 8:36–37.)

The pride condemned in the scriptures is the pride of
self-satisfaction and the pride of comparison.

The pride of self-satisfaction is the opposite of humility.
This attitude insulates us from learning and separates us
from God. This is probably what the Apostles Peter and
James meant when they declared that "God resisteth the

109

proud, but giveth grace unto the humble'' (James 4:6; 1 Peter 5:5).

The pride of comparison is an attitude of superiority toward other people as a result of comparing our possessions, position, or attributes with theirs. The pride of comparison is the opposite of love. This attitude separates us from our fellowmen and leads us toward oppression and persecution. This is probably why the inspired author of Proverbs, in listing the six things the Lord hates, put "a proud look" at the head of a list that also included such oppressive acts as "a lying tongue, and hands that shed innocent blood" (Proverbs 6:17). Like other attitudes that prevent us from having a pure heart, the pride of comparison leads to evil acts.

CHAPTER SEVEN

SPIRITUALITY

The pure in heart have a distinctive way of look-
ing at life. Their attitudes and desires cause
them to view their experiences in terms of eternity. This
eternal perspective affects their choices and priorities. As
they draw farther from worldliness they feel closer to our
Father in Heaven and more able to be guided by his Spirit.
We call this state of mind, this quality of life, *spirituality*.

Spirituality is a lens through which we view life and a
gauge by which we evaluate it. The Apostle Paul expressed
this thought in several of his letters. His second letter to the
Corinthians refers to how we see life:

> We look not at the things which are seen, but at the things
> which are not seen: for the things which are seen are tem-
> poral; but the things which are not seen are eternal (2 Corin-
> thians 4:18).

Paul's letter to the Romans describes how we evaluate our
experiences:

How we interpret our experiences is a function of our degree of spirituality. Some interpret mortality solely in terms of worldly accomplishments and possessions. In contrast, those who have a testimony of the gospel of Jesus Christ should interpret their experiences in terms of their knowledge of the purpose of life, the mission of our Savior, and the eternal destiny of the children of God.

> For they that are after the flesh do mind the things of the flesh; but they that are after the Spirit the things of the Spirit.
> For to be carnally minded is death; but to be spiritually minded is life and peace. (Romans 8:5–6.)

To be spiritually minded is to view and evaluate experiences in terms of the enlarged perspective of eternity.

Each of us has a personal lens through which we *view* the world. Our lens gives its special tint to all we see. It can also suppress some features and emphasize others. It can reveal things otherwise invisible. Through the lens of spirituality, we can know "the things of God" by "the Spirit of God" (1 Corinthians 2:11). As the Apostle Paul taught, such things are "foolishness" to the "natural man." He cannot see them "because they are spiritually discerned" (1 Corinthians 2:14).

As we mature spiritually we come to see things previously unseen. Arthur Henry King describes the process:

> We look at a picture throughout our lives, we listen to a piece of music throughout our lives, we read a book time and again throughout our lives, as we should do—especially the scriptures—and it is different each time. Something else comes in. We see something else there that we never saw before, because we are a different person each time we experience a

work of art. (*The Abundance of the Heart* [Salt Lake City: Bookcraft, 1986], p. 259.)

The scriptures do not change, but what we can see changes in them because we have changed. The same thing happens with the teachings of Church leaders and with personal experiences that mean nothing to the "natural man" but are of eternal significance to the person by whom they are "spiritually discerned."

How we *interpret* our experiences is also a function of our degree of spirituality. Some interpret mortality solely in terms of worldly accomplishments and possessions. These are the interpretations involved in materialism and pride, as discussed in chapters 5 and 6. In contrast, those who have a testimony of the gospel of Jesus Christ should interpret their experiences in terms of their knowledge of the purpose of life, the mission of our Savior, and the eternal destiny of the children of God.

Spirituality is not a function of occupation or calling. A scientist may be more spiritual than a theologian; a teacher may be more spiritual than a supervisor. Spirituality is a state of mind. It is a function of personal attitudes and desires and a determinant of personal priorities. Our degree of spirituality is evident in our words and actions.

Elder John Taylor showed his spirituality in these words, uttered as he reported his mission to Europe in 1852:

Some people have said to me, sometimes, Are you not afraid to cross over the seas, and deserts, where there are wolves and bears, and other ferocious animals. . . . Are you not afraid that you will drop by the way, and leave your body on the desert track, or beneath the ocean's wave? No. Who cares anything about it? What of it, if we should happen to drop by the way? . . . These things don't trouble me, but I have felt to rejoice all the day long, that God has revealed the principle of eternal life, that I am put in possession of that truth, and that I am counted worthy to engage in the work of the Lord. (*Journal of Discourses* 1:17.)

The scriptures often describe degrees of spirituality by metaphors using the word *heart*. The Bible says that when the prophet Samuel anointed Saul to be king over Israel, "God gave [Saul] another heart" (1 Samuel 10:9). Referring to his brothers, Nephi wrote that he was "grieved because of the hardness of their hearts" (1 Nephi 15:4). Paul described the spiritually insensitive by saying, "But even unto this day, when Moses is read, the vail is upon their heart" (2 Corinthians 3:15).

After Alma the Younger was converted, he described spirituality in terms of a change of heart. He said that his father preached to the people, and they "awoke unto God" (Alma 5:7) and "a mighty change was also wrought in their hearts" (Alma 5:13). Then he asked the people of his day a question that can serve as a measure of spirituality in any day or time:

> And now behold, I ask of you, my brethren of the church, have ye spiritually been born of God? Have ye received his image in your countenances? Have ye experienced this mighty change in your hearts? (Alma 5:14.)

Helaman declares that "faith and repentance bringeth a change of heart" (Helaman 15:7).

In another passage, the Book of Mormon describes a people whose faith in Christ filled their souls with joy and consolation, "yea, even to the purifying and the sanctification of their hearts, which sanctification cometh because of their yielding their hearts unto God" (Helaman 3:35). This expression—yielding their hearts unto God—is one of the scripture's most expressive and challenging descriptions of spirituality.

Jacob valued the spiritual, while Esau sought the things of the world. When he was hungry, Esau sold his birthright for a mess of pottage. "Behold," he explained, "I am at the point to die: and what profit shall this birthright do to me?" Many Esaus have given up something of eternal value in order to satisfy a momentary hunger for the things of the world.

In contrast, numerous passages in the Book of Mormon describe the opposite of spirituality as a "hardness of heart." Thus, in the book of Ether we read:

> But behold, the Spirit of the Lord had ceased striving with them, and Satan had full power over the hearts of the people; for they were given up unto the hardness of their hearts, and the blindness of their minds (Ether 15:19).

The prophets who chronicled the wickedest times in Nephite history usually referred to the hardness of the hearts of the people, and to Satan "get[ting] hold upon the hearts of the children of men" (Helaman 6:30; see also Helaman 6:35; 7:15; Mormon 3:12; 4:11). Similarly, the Lord told the Prophet Joseph Smith that Satan "hath put it into [the] hearts" of wicked men to attempt to frustrate the work of the Restoration, and "Satan has great hold upon their hearts; he stirreth them up to iniquity against that which is good" (D&C 10:10, 20). As we read in the Book of Mormon, "Behold, there are many that harden their hearts against the Holy Spirit, that it hath no place in them" (2 Nephi 33:2; see also Alma 12:9–11).

The scriptures contain great illustrations of spirituality as it relates to everyday living. One of these tells of the Savior's arrival at a particular village:

And a certain woman named Martha received him into her house.

And she had a sister called Mary, which also sat at Jesus' feet, and heard his word.

But Martha was cumbered about much serving, and came to him, and said, Lord, dost thou not care that my sister hath left me to serve alone? bid her therefore that she help me.

And Jesus answered and said unto her, Martha, Martha, thou art careful and troubled about many things:

But one thing is needful: and Mary hath chosen that good part, which shall not be taken away from her. (Luke 10:38–42.)

This scripture reminds every Martha, male and female, that we should not be so occupied with what is routine and temporal that we fail to cherish those opportunities that are unique and spiritual.

The contrast between the spiritual and the temporal is also illustrated by the twins Esau and Jacob and their different attitudes toward the birthright. The first-born, Esau, "despised" his birthright (Genesis 25:34). Jacob, the second twin, desired it. Jacob valued the spiritual, while Esau sought the things of the world. When he was hungry, Esau sold his birthright for a mess of pottage. "Behold," he explained, "I am at the point to die: and what profit shall this birthright do to me?" (Genesis 25:32). Many Esaus have given up something of eternal value in order to satisfy a momentary hunger for the things of the world.

The Roman soldiers of Pilate provided an unforgettable illustration of the different perspectives of the carnal mind and the spiritual mind. During a tragic but glorious afternoon on Calvary, a handful of soldiers waited at the foot of a cross. One of the supreme events in all eternity was taking place on the cross above their heads. Oblivious to that fact, they occupied themselves by casting lots to divide the earthly property of the dying Son of God (see

What we see around us depends on what we seek in life. The enemies of the young prophet, Joseph Smith, hounded him in an effort to get possession of the golden plates from which he was to translate the Book of Mormon. They sought the golden plates to get money, not a message. The temporal value of the plates had a price; their spiritual value was priceless.

Matthew 27:35; Luke 23:34: John 19:24). Their example reminds each of us that we should not be casting our lots for the things of the world while the things of eternity, including our families and the work of the Lord, suffer for our lack of attention.

In a BYU devotional several years ago, Elder Loren C. Dunn gave a striking example of a spiritual and a temporal evaluation of an everyday experience. He described how his father, a busy stake president in Tooele, gave his two young sons the responsibility of raising cows on the family farm. The boys had large latitude in what they could do, and they made some mistakes. These were observed by an alert neighbor, who complained to their father about what the young cow-raisers were doing. "Jim, you don't understand," President Dunn replied. "You see, I'm raising boys, not cows." ("Our Spiritual Heritage," *Brigham Young University 1981–82 Fireside and Devotional Speeches* [Provo, Utah: BYU University Publications, 1983], p. 138.) What a marvelous insight! What an example for parents who are inclined to view and evaluate their children's performance solely in temporal terms!

A spiritual evaluation will generally be positive, not negative. In contrast to the prevailing attitude of our day, President Gordon B. Hinckley has urged "that each of us turn from the negativism that so permeates our society and look for the remarkable good among those with whom we associate" (*Ensign*, April 1986, p. 4).

What we *see* around us depends on what we *seek* in life. The Spanish conquerors took irreplaceable objects of art from the craftsmen of the New World and melted them down into gold bullion. The enemies of the young prophet, Joseph Smith, hounded him in an effort to get possession of the golden plates from which he was to translate the Book of Mormon. They sought the golden plates to get money, not a message. The temporal value of the plates had a price; their spiritual value was priceless.

When we understand spirituality, we have no difficulty in understanding Paul's explanation of why Moses renounced his potential birthright in Pharaoh's court:

> Choosing rather to suffer affliction with the people of God, than to enjoy the pleasures of sin for a season;
> Esteeming the reproach of Christ greater riches than the treasures in Egypt. (Hebrews 11:25–26.)

The age-old contrast is between those who have God's law in their hearts and "delight to do [his] will" (Psalm 40:8) and those who "have pleasure" in wickedness (Romans 1:32).

Elder John A. Widtsoe taught that "there is a spiritual meaning of all human acts and earthly events." He continued:

> It is the business of man to find the spiritual meaning of earthly things. . . . No man is quite so happy . . . as he who backs all his labors by such a spiritual interpretation and understanding of the acts of his life. (Conference Report, April 1922, pp. 96–97.)

The Latter-day Saint men and women who settled the Intermountain West acted upon that principle. Judged in terms of the values and aspirations of the world, some pioneer enterprises were failures. The Iron Mission did not succeed in making significant quantities of iron. The Cotton Mission did not give the Utah Territory self-sufficiency in cotton production. Efforts to manufacture sugar did not achieve material success for forty years. The Perpetual Emigration Fund did not perpetuate itself because many immigrants were unable to pay their debt to it. (See Leonard J. Arrington, *Great Basin Kingdom* [Lincoln, Nebraska: University of Nebraska, 1966], pp. 116–27, 217–22, 386–91.) But, when measured against the eternal values of loyalty, cooperation, and consecration, some of the most conspicuous worldly failures are seen as the pioneer enterprisers' greatest triumphs. Whatever their financial outcome, these enterprises called forth the sacrifices that molded pioneers into Saints and prepared Saints for exaltation. Unto God, "all things . . . are spiritual" (D&C 29:34).

In another great event in Mormon history, several hundred men marched from Ohio to give military relief to the persecuted Saints in Zion—western Missouri. But when the men of Zion's Camp approached their intended destination, the Prophet Joseph Smith disbanded them. According to its ostensible purpose, the expedition was a failure. But most of the men who were to lead the Church for the next half-century, including those who would take the Saints across the plains and colonize the Intermountain West, came to know the Prophet Joseph and received their formative leadership training in the march of Zion's Camp. As Elder Orson F. Whitney said of Zion's Camp:

> The redemption of Zion is more than the purchase or recovery of lands, the building of cities, or even the founding of nations. It is the conquest of the heart, the subjugation of the soul, the sanctifying of the flesh, the purifying and ennobling of the passions. (Orson F. Whitney, *The Life of Heber C. Kimball* [Salt Lake City: Bookcraft, 1945], p. 65.)

As is evident from these examples, writers and readers of Church history divide along an axis of spirituality. Criticisms of religious institutions or religious-motivated behavior are often rooted in an unstated rejection of the value or importance of religion. President Gordon B. Hinckley analyzed these critics:

> Wearing the spectacles of humanism, they fail to realize that spiritual emotions, with recognition of the influence of the Holy Spirit, had as much to do with the actions of our forebears as did the processes of the mind. They have failed to realize that religion is as much concerned with the heart as it is with the intellect. ("The Continuing Pursuit of Truth," *Ensign*, April 1986, p. 5.)

The first of the Ten Commandments—"Thou shalt have no other gods before me" (Exodus 20:3)—epitomizes the nature of spirituality. A spiritual person has no priorities ahead of God. A person who seeks or serves other objectives, such as power or prominence, is not spiritual.

In teaching that we must be ready to abandon all for the sake of the kingdom, the Savior said: "And whosoever doth not bear his cross, and come after me, cannot be my disciple. Wherefore, settle this thing in your hearts, that ye will do the things which I shall teach, and command you. (JST, Luke 14:27–28.)

Jeremiah used the same figure of speech in protesting his spirituality to the Lord: "Thou, O Lord, knowest me: thou hast seen me, and tried mine heart toward thee" (Jeremiah 12:3).

Elder James E. Faust reminds us of the power of spirituality:

> The strengthening of the inner self must come about by the Saints' being strengthened spiritually. The admonition to the Galatians was: "For he that soweth to his flesh shall of the flesh reap corruption; but he that soweth to the Spirit shall of the Spirit reap life everlasting." (Galatians 6:8.)
>
> Problems will yield to a spiritual solution, for the higher laws involve the spiritual; the Lord said: "All things unto me

are spiritual, and not at any time have I given unto you a law which was temporal." (D&C 29:34.) (*To Reach Even Unto You* [Salt Lake City: Deseret Book Co., 1980], p. 13.)

The primacy of the spiritual over the temporal is also stressed in the teachings of the Savior's three senior Apostles. Peter taught, "All flesh is as grass, and all the glory of man as the flower of grass. The grass withereth, and the flower thereof falleth away: but the word of the Lord endureth for ever." (1 Peter 1:24.)

James asked: "Know ye not that the friendship of the world is enmity with God? whosoever therefore will be a friend of the world is the enemy of God." (James 4:4.)

The Apostle John wrote:

Love not the world, neither the things that are in the world. If any man love the world, the love of the Father is not in him.

For all that is in the world, the lust of the flesh, and the lust of the eyes, and the pride of life, is not of the Father, but is of the world.

And the world passeth away, and the lust thereof: but he that doeth the will of God abideth for ever. (1 John 2:15–17.)

As noted in chapter 5, the most important thing about money and property is the attitude with which we view and manage them. If allowed to become an object of worship or priority, money and property can make us selfish and prideful, "puffed up . . . with the vain things of the world" (Alma 31:27). In contrast, if used for fulfilling our legal obligations and for paying our tithes and offerings, money can demonstrate integrity and develop unselfishness. The spiritually enlightened use of property can help prepare us for the higher law of a celestial glory. "Wherefore," as Jacob taught, "do not spend money for that which is of no worth, nor your labor for that which cannot satisfy" (2 Nephi 9:51).

Perhaps some of women's apparent superiority in
spirituality is because historically they have remained
in the home, less exposed to the anti-spiritual
influences of the world than their male counterparts. If
so, as more women are employed and exposed to anti-
spiritual influences outside the home, they will need to
make increased efforts to preserve and develop their
spirituality.

The qualities of spirituality that persons have been able
to embody in their lives are often evident in the way they
react to death or other apparent tragedies or misfortunes.
Faithful Latter-day Saints can bear the death of loved ones
because they have faith in the resurrection and the eternal
nature of family ties. And they can repent and rise above
their mistakes and inadequacies because they know that
our Savior "suffered these things for all, that they might
not suffer if they would repent" (D&C 19:16).

Seen with the perspective of eternity, a temporal set-
back can be an opportunity to develop soul-power of
eternal significance. Strength is forged in adversity. Faith
is developed in a setting where we cannot see what lies
ahead.

Lehi promised his son Jacob that God "shall consecrate
thine afflictions for thy gain" (2 Nephi 2:2). In the midst of
the Missouri persecutions the Lord assured the Saints that
"all things wherewith you have been afflicted shall work
together for your good" (D&C 98:3). As the Prophet
Joseph Smith neared despair in his sufferings in Liberty
Jail, the voice of the Lord gave comfort in declaring that
"all these things shall give thee experience, and shall be
for thy good" (D&C 122:7). Those who can look upon their
afflictions in this manner have spirituality.

Spirituality comes more naturally to some than to others. Spirituality is a spiritual gift.

I am persuaded that women are generally more spiritual than men. Perhaps this is because their unique gift of child-bearing, which places them at the wellspring of life, makes them more sensitive to eternal verities. Perhaps some of women's apparent superiority in spirituality is because historically they have remained in the home, less exposed to the anti-spiritual influences of the world than their male counterparts. If so, as more women are employed and exposed to anti-spiritual influences outside the home, they will need to make increased efforts to preserve and develop their spirituality.

How do we achieve spirituality? How do we attain that degree of holiness wherein we can have the constant companionship of the Holy Ghost and view and evaluate the things of this world with the perspective of eternity?

We seek spirituality through faith, repentance, and baptism; through forgiveness of one another; through fasting and prayer; through righteous desires and pure thoughts and actions. We seek spirituality through service to our fellowmen; through worship; through feasting on the word of God, in the scriptures and in the teachings of the living prophets. We attain spirituality through making and keeping covenants with the Lord, through conscientiously trying to keep all the commandments of God. Spirituality is not acquired suddenly. It is the consequence of a succession of right choices. It is the harvest of a righteous life.

Through the lens of spirituality we see all the commandments of God as invitations to blessings. Obedience and sacrifice, loyalty and love, fidelity and family, all appear in eternal perspective. The words of the Savior, as given to the world in Joseph Smith's inspired translation, have renewed significance:

And whosoever will lose his life in this world, for my sake, shall find it in the world to come.

Therefore, forsake the world, and save your souls; for what is a man profited, if he shall gain the whole world, and lose his own soul? Or what shall a man give in exchange for his soul? (JST, Matthew 16:28–29.)

The prophet Mormon explained one consequence of the faith that accompanies spirituality: "Angels . . . minister unto the children of men. For behold, they are subject unto [Christ], to minister according to the word of his command, showing themselves unto them of strong faith and a firm mind in every form of godliness." (Moroni 7:29–30.)

The ultimate fruits of spirituality were revealed to the Prophet Joseph Smith in section 88 of the Doctrine and Covenants:

Truth abideth and hath no end; and if it be in you it shall abound.

And if your eye be single to my glory, your whole bodies shall be filled with light, and there shall be no darkness in you; and that body which is filled with light comprehendeth all things.

Therefore, sanctify yourselves that your minds become single to God. (D&C 88:66–68.)

Those whose minds are single to God are pure in heart.

CHAPTER EIGHT

WORSHIP

In every age God has commanded his children to worship him. (See Moses 1:17; Moses 5:5; Exodus 34:14; Mosiah 18:25; Matthew 4:10; Luke 4:8.) Modern revelation reemphasizes "that all men must repent and believe on the name of Jesus Christ, and worship the Father in his name. . . . or they cannot be saved in the kingdom of God" (D&C 20:29).

Worship often includes actions, but true worship always involves a particular attitude of mind.

The attitude of worship evokes the deepest feelings of allegiance, adoration, and awe. Worship combines love and reverence in a state of devotion that draws our spirits closer to God. President Spencer W. Kimball said that the reason God commanded us to worship him is that this would bring us closer to him (*The Teachings of Spencer W. Kimball* [Salt Lake City: Bookcraft, 1982], p. 30).

Jesus taught that we should worship the Father "in spirit and in truth" (John 4:23–24). He spoke these words after the Samaritan woman sought to engage him in controversy over whether people ought to worship in Jerusalem or on Mount Gerizim in Samaria. Declining to discuss that subject, Jesus addressed the woman with a statement that focused attention on the real issue: "Ye worship ye know not what; we know what we worship; and salvation is of the Jews" (JST, John 4:24).

The Savior explained further:

> But the hour cometh, and now is, when the true worshippers shall worship the Father in spirit and in truth: for the Father seeketh such to worship him.
>
> For unto such hath God promised his Spirit. And they who worship him, must worship him in spirit and in truth. (JST, John 4:25–26.)

In order to worship "in spirit," we must have the right attitude of mind. We must know *how* to worship. In order to worship "in truth," we must know *what* we worship.

An episode recorded in the Book of Mormon shows the importance of knowing what we worship. The Zoramites worshipped a god who was a spirit and would be a spirit forever, who had made known to them that there would be no Christ, and who had "elected" them that they all would be saved (see Alma 31:15–17). From this description it appears that the Zoramites were, knowingly or unknowingly, worshipping the person and plan of Satan.

Elder James E. Talmage taught: "Man's capacity for worship is a measure of his comprehension of God. The fuller the acquaintance and the closer the communion between the worshipper and Deity, the more thorough and sincere will be his homage." (*The Articles of Faith* [Salt Lake City: The Church of Jesus Christ of Latter-day Saints, 1924], pp. 395–96.)

We worship God the Father, the great Elohim. Though there be "gods many, and lords many" (1 Corinthians

Although there are actions that we associate with worship, no act constitutes worship unless it is accompanied by a particular state of mind, the attitude of worship. True worshippers, as Jesus taught, "must worship [him] in spirit and in truth."

8:5), his position is unique. He is the Father of our spirits, the creator of all things, and the author of our salvation. God taught Moses: "Mine Only Begotten is and shall be the Savior, for he is full of grace and truth; but there is no God beside me" (Moses 1:6). As the object of our worship, God the Eternal Father "stands supreme and alone." ("Only One God to Worship," *Improvement Era* [April, 1912], 15:483–85; also in *Messages of the First Presidency*, ed. James R. Clark [Salt Lake City: Bookcraft, 1970], 4:270–71. See D&C 20:17–19.) The Apostle Paul declared: "To us there is but one God, the Father, of whom are all things, and we in him; and one Lord Jesus Christ, by whom are all things, and we by him" (1 Corinthians 8:6).

We also worship the Lord Jesus Christ, the Son of God, the Great Jehovah, the Holy One of Israel (see Bruce R. McConkie, *The Promised Messiah* [Salt Lake City: Deseret Book Co., 1978], pp. 562–66). At the direction of God the Father, the Son accomplished the work of creation, spoke with the prophets, and completed the glorious work of redemption. We worship him as our Savior and our Redeemer. The scriptures sometimes refer to him as the Father, because when we have claimed the benefit of his atoning sacrifice by obedience to the laws and ordinances of the gospel and he has redeemed us from our sins, we become his spiritually begotten sons and daughters (Mosiah 5:7–8; 15:10–12).

How do we worship? Examples of worship in action include prayers, sermons, testimonies, gospel study, service, and singing. For example, who has not thrilled with the singing of "Oh, Come, All Ye Faithful"? Each verse has a thrilling, worshipful message, but none more beautiful than this conclusion:

> Yea, Lord, we greet thee, born this happy morning;
>> Jesus, to thee be all glory given.
> Son of the Father, now in flesh appearing;
>> Oh, come, let us adore him;
>> Oh, come let us adore him;
>> Oh, come, let us adore him, Christ, the Lord.
>> (*Hymns*, 1985, no. 202.)

We also perform acts of worship when we obey the commandments of God. Elder Bruce R. McConkie called obedience "the true measure of true worship" (*Mormon Doctrine*, 2d ed. [Salt Lake City: Bookcraft, 1966], p. 849).

Although there are *actions* that we associate with worship, no act constitutes worship unless it is accompanied by a particular state of mind, the *attitude* of worship. True worshippers, as Jesus taught, "must worship [him] in spirit and in truth" (JST, John 4:26). The prophet Nephi described the blessings that would come to the lost sheep of the house of Israel, "when that day shall come that they shall believe in Christ, and worship the Father in his name, with pure hearts and clean hands" (2 Nephi 25:16). Then Nephi commanded: "Ye must bow down before him, and worship him with all your might, mind, and strength, and your whole soul" (2 Nephi 25:29). This echoes what the prophet Moses taught Israel: "But if from thence thou shalt seek the Lord thy God, thou shalt find him, if thou seek him with all thy heart and with all thy soul" (Deuteronomy 4:29).

"Worship is the voluntary homage of the soul. Under compulsion, or for purposes of display, one may insincerely perform all the outward ceremonies of an established style of adoration; he may voice words of prescribed prayers; his lips may profess a creed; yet his effort is but a mockery of worship and its indulgence a sin. God asks no reluctant homage nor unwilling praise."

Elder James E. Talmage taught that a person who has the true and heartfelt attitude of worship can worship without outward action:

> Worship is not a matter of form any more than is prayer. It consists not in posture, in gesture, in ritual or in creed. Worship most profound may be rendered with none of the artificial accessories of ritualistic service. (*The Articles of Faith*, p. 396.)

Neither is worship a matter of place. The prophet Alma condemned the Zoramites' limitation of worship to set prayers offered from a holy stand in the center of their synagogues (see Alma 31:12–21; 33:1–9). His companion, Amulek, taught that they should humble themselves "and worship God, in whatsoever place ye may be in" (Alma 34:38).

Worship cannot be forced, and it is not casual or indifferent. Worship requires the wholehearted intent of a loving spirit. Worship, like prayer, is the soul's sincere desire:

> Worship is the voluntary homage of the soul. Under compulsion, or for purposes of display, one may insincerely perform all the outward ceremonies of an established style of adoration; he may voice words of prescribed prayers; his lips

may profess a creed; yet his effort is but a mockery of worship and its indulgence a sin. God asks no reluctant homage nor unwilling praise.

Continuing, Elder Talmage explains the importance of the inward desire:

> Formalism in worship is acceptable only so far as it is accompanied by an intelligent devoutness; and it is genuine only as it is an aid to the spiritual devotion that leads to communion with Deity. The spoken prayer is but empty sound if it be anything less than an index to the volume of the soul's righteous desire. (James E. Talmage, *The Articles of Faith*, p. 397.)

Actions that we associate with worship, while not constituting worship in themselves, suggest the attitude of mind that constitutes true worship. Such actions include kneeling, bowing the head, professing faith, and participating in public worship services.

Scriptural accounts of worshippers often describe their bowing down before the Lord. When the wise men came from the east and found the young child with Mary his mother, they "fell down, and worshipped him" (Matthew 2:11). In vision, Nephi "saw many fall down at [the Savior's] feet and worship him" (1 Nephi 11:24). When the disciples saw the risen Lord, they "held him by the feet, and worshipped him" (Matthew 28:9). When the Savior appeared to the people on this continent,

> they did cry out with one accord, saying:
> Hosanna! Blessed be the name of the Most High God! And they did fall down at the feet of Jesus, and did worship him. . . .
> And Nephi . . . went forth, and bowed himself before the Lord and did kiss his feet. (3 Nephi 11:16–19. See also 3 Nephi 17:10; D&C 18:40.)

Professions of faith and testimony are also acts of worship. There are many such in the scriptures. After the Sermon on the Mount, "There came a leper and worshipped him, saying, Lord, if thou wilt, thou canst make me clean" (Matthew 8:2). After Jesus had calmed the waves and walked upon the water, "Then they that were in the ship came and worshipped him, saying; Of a truth thou art the Son of God" (Matthew 14:33). A gentile woman whose daughter was vexed with a devil "worshipped him, saying, Lord, help me" (Matthew 15:25). After he had healed a blind man on the Sabbath, Jesus introduced himself as the Son of God and the man replied, "Lord, I believe. And he worshipped him." (John 9:38.)

The most familiar acts of worship take place in public worship services. Perhaps because of that familiarity, many worshippers fail to get far enough beyond the level of mere attendance to make their worship a matter of attitude and spirit. To worship in spirit requires preparation. Elder Mark E. Petersen advised that we should "cleanse ourselves in preparation for that [Sabbath] worship by confessing our sins and repenting of them" ("The Sabbath Day," *Ensign*, May 1975, p. 49).

The sacrament has the central place in our public worship. Elder David B. Haight has taught: "Associated with the partaking of the sacrament are principles that are fundamental to man's advancement and exaltation in the Kingdom of God and the shaping of one's spiritual character" ("The Sacrament," *Ensign*, May 1983, p. 14).

Partaking of the sacrament is an act, but each portion of the sacrament service carries strong emphasis that this form of worship requires a particular attitude of mind.

We begin with a sacrament hymn. These two verses of "Jesus of Nazareth, Savior and King" are illustrative of the worshipful thoughts and attitudes that sacrament hymns encourage in those who participate:

While of this broken bread humbly we eat,
Our thoughts to thee are led in rev'rence sweet.

131

"We attend sacrament meetings to worship the Lord. If the meeting is conducted or if we attend with any other thought, we have missed the spirit of the occasion. Those who attend meeting only when the speaker is eloquent, the lecturer is noted, or the music is excellent, are far afield of the high purpose and loftiness of this meeting in the house of prayer. It should be worship from the first announcement to the final prayer."

Bruised, broken, torn for us on Calvary's hill—
Thy suff'ring borne for us lives with us still.

As to our lips the cup gently we press,
Our hearts are lifted up, thy name we bless!
Guide us where'er we go, till in the end
Life evermore we'll know through thee, our Friend.
(*Hymns*, 1985, no. 181.)

Next, the elder or priest blesses the emblems of the sacrament. His prayers should be audible to all who will partake. He prays to God the Eternal Father that all who will partake of the bread "may eat in remembrance of the body of thy Son," and that all who drink of the water "may do it in remembrance of the blood of thy Son, which was shed for them" (D&C 20:77, 79).

During the passing of the sacrament, we all have the opportunity to worship by pondering on the sacrifice of the Son of God, who suffered and died for our sins and who is our Savior and Redeemer.

In order for the act of partaking of the sacrament to constitute an act of worship, it must be done with the "remembrance" specified in these prayers of the priesthood holders who officiate at this sacred ordinance. This is clear from the following revelation, given in the first year of the restored Church:

> For, behold, I say unto you, that it mattereth not what ye shall eat or what ye shall drink when ye partake of the sacrament, if it so be that ye do it with an eye single to my glory—remembering unto the Father my body which was laid down for you, and my blood which was shed for the remission of your sins (D&C 27:2).

Though worship may be encouraged and informed by meeting with others, true worship is an individual act and an individual responsibility. Worship occurs in the mind of the worshipper. President Spencer W. Kimball taught this principle of individual responsibility with this memorable example:

> We attend sacrament meetings to worship the Lord. If the meeting is conducted or if we attend with any other thought, we have missed the spirit of the occasion. Those who attend meeting only when the speaker is eloquent, the lecturer is noted, or the music is excellent, are far afield of the high purpose and loftiness of this meeting in the house of prayer. It should be worship from the first announcement to the final prayer, consisting of the singing of sacred songs, prayers of gratitude, the partaking of the sacrament with appropriate thoughts, and the expounding of the gospel and bearing testimony of its divinity. . . .
>
> . . . Worship is an individual matter. The best choir, the best speaker, the most noted lecturer, cannot bring true worship into your soul. It must proceed from within, out of a deep sense of love and devotion and dependence and humility. . . .
>
> One good but mistaken man I know claimed he could get more out of a good book on Sunday than he could get in attending church services, saying that the sermons were hardly up to his standards. But we do not go to Sabbath meetings to be entertained or even solely to be instructed. We

"The more enlightened member of the Church goes to church in order to give, to give strength, to feed, to inspire, to help. . . . They sit in the congregation and pray intently for the speaker. They find that as they do so in a sacrament meeting that the Lord will speak to them using that speaker, however weak he may be in his knowledge and understanding of the gospel, to open additional spiritual doors for the one seated praying."

---

go to worship the Lord. It is an individual responsibility, and regardless of what is said from the pulpit, if one wishes to worship the Lord in spirit and in truth, he may do so by attending his meetings, partaking of the sacrament, and contemplating the beauties of the gospel. If the service is a failure to you, you have failed. No one can worship for you; you must do your own waiting upon the Lord. (*The Teachings of Spencer W. Kimball* [Salt Lake City: Bookcraft, 1982], pp. 514–15.)

Elder Gene R. Cook expresses this same principle in terms of an attitude of giving:

The more enlightened member of the Church goes to church in order *to give, to give strength, to feed, to inspire, to help.* . . . They sit in the congregation and pray intently for the speaker. They find that as they do so in a sacrament meeting that the Lord will speak to them using that speaker, however weak he may be in his knowledge and understanding of the gospel, to open additional spiritual doors for the one seated praying.

The speaker, for example, may mention the concept of faith and give the most elemental description of what it is. The faithful man in the audience is praying to help him, the speaker, and listening intently to what is said. If he so does, the Lord will open up numerous other more profound ideas about faith to the one praying for instruction from the real source of all learning, namely the Lord. (Unpublished memorandum, "The Purpose of the Church," February 24, 1985.)

The purpose of worship is to draw closer to God, in order to enlarge our knowledge of him and strengthen our efforts to keep his commandments.

The effects of perfect worship are described by Elder Bruce R. McConkie:

> Perfect worship is emulation. We honor those whom we imitate. The most perfect way of worship is to be holy as Jehovah is holy. It is to be pure as Christ is pure. It is to do the things that enable us to become like the Father. The course is one of obedience, of living by every word that proceedeth from the mouth of God, of keeping the commandments.
>
> How do we worship the Lord? We do it by going from grace to grace, until we receive the fulness of the Father and are glorified in light and truth as is the case with our Pattern and Prototype, the Promised Messiah. (*The Promised Messiah*, pp. 568–69.)

In the remarkable revelation known as section 93 of the Doctrine and Covenants, the Lord revealed a portion of the truths recorded in the record of John. The Lord explained that he gave this knowledge to his children in this dispensation "that you may understand and know how to worship, and know what you worship" (D&C 93:19). John recorded the premortal existence of Christ, his role in the creation, his mortal ministry, and his continuing "from grace to grace, until he received a fulness" (D&C 93:13). John then bore record that the Only Begotten of the Father "received a fulness of the glory of the Father," including "all power, both in heaven and on earth" (D&C 93:16–17). This knowledge of the exaltation of the Son tells us "what" we worship. It also tells us "how" to worship and *why* we worship:

That you may come unto the Father in my name, and in due time receive of his fulness.

For if you keep my commandments you shall receive of his fulness, and be glorified in me as I am in the Father; therefore, I say unto you, you shall receive grace for grace. (D&C 93:19–20.)

In truth, as God revealed to his prophet, Moses, "This is my work and my glory—to bring to pass the immortality and eternal life of man" (Moses 1:39). That is the object and end of worship.

CHAPTER NINE

SEEKING A PURE HEART

Preceding chapters have explored the importance of motives, desires, and attitudes. The scriptures and the teachings of modern prophets contain hundreds of illustrations—many of which are reviewed here—of the significance of what the Apostle Paul called "the inner man" (Ephesians 3:16).

The word most commonly used to describe the condition of the inner man is *heart*. Alma referred to the kind of conversion that led to the salvation of a people as "a mighty change . . . wrought in their hearts" (Alma 5:13). To be "pure in heart" is to achieve that condition in which motives, desires, and attitudes are acceptable to God and consistent with the eternal progress that is the ultimate destiny of his children.

This concluding chapter concentrates on how we can seek to become pure in heart. It concerns how we can achieve the right attitudes and priorities, how we can control our thoughts, and how we can acquire good motives and desires.

The issue is not what we have done but what we have become. And what we have become is the result of more than our actions. It is also the result of our attitudes, our motives, and our desires. Each of these is an ingredient of the pure heart.

The Importance of Being Pure in Heart

In the second chapter of Romans, the Apostle Paul teaches that God will "judge the secrets of men" (Romans 2:16). His judgment will be "according to truth" (Romans 2:2). In describing that judgment Paul contrasted the position of those Jews who preached the law and then did not practice it with Gentiles who did not have the law but whose actions "shew the work of the law written in their hearts" (Romans 2:15). He concluded his example with this teaching:

> For he is not a Jew, which is one outwardly; neither is that circumcision, which is outward in the flesh:
>
> But he is a Jew, which is one inwardly; and circumcision is that of the heart, in the spirit, and not in the letter; whose praise is not of men, but of God. (Romans 2:28–29.)

To paraphrase, a person is a true Latter-day Saint if he (or she) is so *inwardly*, if his conversion is that of the heart, in the spirit, whose praise is not from men for outward acts but from God for the inward desires of his heart.

As we seek to determine whether we have become true Latter-day Saints—inwardly as well as outwardly—it soon becomes apparent that the critical element is progress, not longevity. The question is not how much time we have logged, but how far we have progressed toward perfection. As Elder Neal A. Maxwell has said, "Life is not lineal, but

experiential, not chronological, but developmental"
(*Ensign*, December 1986, p. 23). The issue is not what we
have *done* but what we have *become*. And what we have
become is the result of more than our actions. It is also the
result of our attitudes, our motives, and our desires. Each
of these is an ingredient of the pure heart.

Some persons achieve great progress toward perfection
with just a few of life's experiences. Others seem to pass
through the same experiences again and again and yet remain relatively unchanged by them. The contrast is sug-
gestive of the difference between the status of one person
with four years' experience and another person with one
year's experience repeated twenty times. The question is
not longevity but growth. Growth is not measured by a
clock or an odometer but by what has happened in the
heart.

These truths provide an insight into the parable of the
laborers in the vineyard (see Matthew 20). A householder
"went out early in the morning to hire labourers into his
vineyard" (Matthew 20:1). He agreed to pay them a penny
a day, and sent them to work. He went out again "about
the third hour, and saw others standing idle in the market-
place," hired them, and sent them into his vineyard,
agreeing to pay them "whatsoever is right" (Matthew
20:3–4). He went out at the sixth and the ninth hours "and
did likewise" (Matthew 20:5). Again at the eleventh hour
he "found others standing idle" whom no man had hired
and sent them "also into the vineyard; and whatsoever is
right, that shall ye receive" (Matthew 20:6–7).

When the day was over, the householder instructed his
steward to pay every man the same wage. Those that were
hired at the eleventh hour received the same as those
who had worked all day. When the all-day workers mur-
mured, complaining that those who had worked but one
hour were paid the same as those who had "borne the

**To become pure in heart—to achieve exaltation—we
must alter our attitudes and priorities to a condition of
spirituality, we must control our thoughts, we must
reform our motives, and we must perfect our desires.**

---

burden and heat of the day'' (Matthew 20:12), the householder reminded them that all had been paid the agreed
amount and therefore none had any cause for complaint.

This parable teaches us that the rewards we will receive
in the judgment will not be computed according to the
duration of our service. Exaltation, the ultimate reward of
the Father, is available to all who qualify. (See Bruce R.
McConkie, *Doctrinal New Testament Commentary* [Salt
Lake City: Bookcraft, 1966] 1:561.) Eternal life is "the
greatest of all the gifts of God" (D&C 14:7). None can
receive more than this.

By reason of their willingness and their loyalty to their
master, by the end of the day the laborers hired in the
eleventh hour had become as much—had qualified as com-
pletely—as those who had served the entire period. The
master's rewards were not given for the time served or for
any other external measure. His rewards were for the ultimate and comprehensive internal measure—what the
workers had become within themselves as a result of their
service.

Altering Our Attitudes and Priorities

To become pure in heart—to achieve exaltation—we
must alter our attitudes and priorities to a condition of
spirituality, we must control our thoughts, we must reform
our motives, and we must perfect our desires. How can
this be done?

The first step in the alteration of our attitudes and our priorities is to face up to our own imperfections and the need to change. President Brigham Young emphasized this need for self-examination and self-improvement when he taught the Saints how they should prepare for the prophesied day of vengeance, when the Lord would consume the wicked. "Do not be too anxious for the Lord to hasten his work," he counseled. We should not "be in a hurry to see the overthrow of the wicked." Instead, "Let our anxiety be centered upon this one thing, the sanctification of our own hearts, the purifying of our own affections, the preparing of ourselves for the approach of the events that are hastening upon us." (*Journal of Discourses* 9:3.)

We begin by questioning ourselves. Stripping away our pretenses and our false fronts, probing honestly and deeply within our inner selves, we should seek to identify our true attitudes and priorities.

Alma prescribed this kind of self-examination in his high-priestly teachings. He challenged his people to examine their hearts, and he suggested several key measures of attitude:

> Could ye say, if ye were called to die at this time, within yourselves, that ye have been *sufficiently humble*? . . .
>
> Behold, are ye *stripped of pride*? I say unto you, if ye are not ye are not prepared to meet God . . . and such an one hath not eternal life.
>
> Behold, I say, is there one among you who is not *stripped of envy*? . . . Such an one is not found guiltless.
>
> And again I say unto you, is there one among you that doth *make a mock of his brother*?

Alma concluded by describing the effects of these attitudes on the one who has them:

> Wo unto such an one, for he is not prepared, and the time is at hand that he must repent or he cannot be saved! (Alma 5:27–31; italics added.)

Attitudes and priorities have consequences. Attitudes such as materialism and pride on the one hand or spirituality, humility, and worship on the other hand guide the choices that shape our actions and make us what we are.

Our attitudes determine how we evaluate our life's experiences. They determine how we evaluate ourselves. They also govern how we look at other people. Are we inclined to judge an eternal soul by the appearance of an earthly body? Do we see the beautiful soul of a brother or sister, or do we only see that person's earthly tabernacle? Bodies can be distorted by handicap, twisted by injury, or worn by age. But if we can learn to see the inner man and woman, we will be seeing as God sees, and loving as he loves.

The Book of Mormon lists these attitudes that God "despiseth": "The wise, and the learned, and they that are rich, who are puffed up because of their learning, and their wisdom, and their riches" (2 Nephi 9:42). What God despiseth is not wisdom, learning, or riches, but the attitude of him (or her) who is "puffed up because of [them]." The evil is in the attitude, which is what chapter 6 calls the pride of self-satisfaction.

This same verse of scripture next describes how those who are "puffed up" can still qualify for the promised blessings. They must "cast these things away, and consider themselves fools before God, and come down in the depths of humility" (2 Nephi 9:42). Humility is the opposite of and the antidote for the pride of self-satisfaction. To counter pride we need to cultivate humility.

What chapter 6 calls the pride of comparison is also a matter of attitude. It is also rooted in preoccupation with self. One antidote for that preoccupation is service. Service to others swings our spotlight of priorities outward, away from ourselves. To counter pride we need to give unselfish service.

142

"Developing spirituality and attuning ourselves to the highest influences of godliness is not an easy matter. It takes time and frequently involves a struggle. It will not happen by chance, but is accomplished only through deliberate effort and by calling upon God and keeping his commandments."

The prophet Jacob prescribed another remedy, a thought and an action that can be taken by those afflicted with the pride of comparison because of their riches: "Think of your brethren like unto yourselves, and be familiar with all and free with your substance, that they may be rich like unto you" (Jacob 2:17). To counter this kind of pride we need to be "familiar with all and free with [our] substance."

Differences in knowledge, prominence, or position can also be sources of the pride of comparison. The prophet Alma describes how those Nephites who were "steadfast and immovable in keeping the commandments of God" resisted this kind of pride:

> And when the priests left their labor to impart the word of God unto the people, the people also left their labors to hear the word of God. And when the priest had imparted unto them the word of God they all returned again diligently unto their labors; and the priest, not esteeming himself above his hearers, for the preacher was no better than the hearer, neither was the teacher any better than the learner; and thus they were all equal, and they did all labor, every man according to his strength. (Alma 1:26.)

No matter how prominent or praised, the preacher is no better than the hearer, the teacher is no better than the learner. To avoid pride, preachers and teachers and others in prominent positions must struggle not to esteem themselves above their hearers.

As discussed in chapter 7, the attitude or priority that is most desirable in eternal terms is spirituality.

The degree of spirituality a person has achieved is a measure of his or her progress toward perfection. The acts and thoughts that make us more spiritual move us toward our goal of being pure in heart.

The importance of this subject justifies repeating a key paragraph from chapter 7, which describes how spirituality is achieved:

We seek spirituality through faith, repentance, and baptism; through forgiveness of one another; through fasting and prayer; through righteous desires and pure thoughts and actions. We seek spirituality through service to our fellowmen; through worship; through feasting on the word of God, in the scriptures and in the teachings of the living prophets. We attain spirituality through making and keeping covenants with the Lord, through conscientiously trying to keep all the commandments of God. Spirituality is not acquired suddenly. It is the consequence of a succession of right choices. It is the harvest of a righteous life.

President Howard W. Hunter gave this inspired counsel on the development of spirituality:

> Developing spirituality and attuning ourselves to the highest influences of godliness is not an easy matter. It takes time and frequently involves a struggle. It will not happen by chance, but is accomplished only through deliberate effort and by calling upon God and keeping his commandments. . . .
>
> None of us has attained perfection or the zenith of spiritual growth that is possible in mortality. Every person can and must make spiritual progress. The gospel of Jesus Christ is the divine plan for that spiritual growth eternally. It is more than a code of ethics. It is more than an ideal social order. It is more than positive thinking about self-improve-

ment and determination. The gospel is the saving power of the Lord Jesus Christ with his priesthood and sustenance and with the Holy Spirit. With faith in the Lord Jesus Christ and obedience to his gospel, a step at a time improving as we go, pleading for strength, improving our attitudes and our ambitions, we will find ourselves successfully in the fold of the Good Shepherd. That will require discipline and training and exertion and strength. But as the Apostle Paul said, "I can do all things through Christ which strengtheneth me" (Philippians 4:13). ("Developing Spirituality," *Ensign*, May 1979, pp. 25–26.)

Controlling Our Thoughts

To achieve spirituality and to reform our motives and perfect our desires we must learn to control our thoughts. The prophet Alma taught his faithful son Helaman: "Let all thy thoughts be directed unto the Lord; yea, let the affections of thy heart be placed upon the Lord forever" (Alma 37:36).

In the great revelation given in Liberty Jail, the Lord commanded the Prophet Joseph Smith to conform his thoughts to this high standard: "Let thy bowels also be full of charity towards all men, and to the household of faith, and let virtue garnish thy thoughts unceasingly" (D&C 121:45). This means that in our innermost feelings we should always be "full of [love] towards all men" and that our thoughts should always be garnished with virtue, which is goodness, purity, and truth. The revelation promises us that when we do this our "confidence [shall] wax strong in the presence of God" (D&C 121:45; see also 1 John 3:21).

Two servants of the Lord have given us specific suggestions about how to control our thoughts. Both suggestions involve the banishing of evil thoughts by filling our minds with good ones.

"If you can control your thoughts, you can overcome habits—even degrading, personal habits. If you can learn to master them, you will have a happy life."

President Marion G. Romney taught:

> I am persuaded, my brothers and sisters, that it is irrational to hope to escape the lusts of the world without substituting for them as the subjects of our thoughts the things of the Spirit, and I know that the things of the Spirit are taught with mighty power in the Book of Mormon. . . .
>
> And so, I counsel you, my beloved brothers and sisters and friends everywhere, to make reading the Book of Mormon a few minutes each day a lifelong practice. ("The Book of Mormon," *Ensign*, May 1980, p. 67.)

If we fill our minds with "the things of the Spirit"— things that teach of God or promote that which is pleasing to him, things that are "virtuous, lovely, or of good report or praiseworthy" (Articles of Faith 1:13)—we will be able to control our thoughts within the bounds our Creator has set as the preconditions of spirituality.

Elder Boyd K. Packer gave this memorable suggestion for controlling our thoughts:

> The mind is like a stage—the curtain is always up except when we are asleep. There is always some act being performed on that stage. . . .
>
> Have you noticed that without any real intent on your part, in the middle of almost any performance, a shady little thought may creep in from the wings and attract your attention? . . .
>
> What do you do at a time like that, when the stage of your mind is commandeered by the imps of unclean thinking? Whether they be the gray ones that seem almost clean or the filthy ones that leave no room for doubt?

146

If you can control your thoughts, you can overcome habits —even degrading, personal habits. If you can learn to master them, you will have a happy life.

I would teach you this. Choose from among the sacred music of the Church a favorite hymn, one with words that are uplifting and music that is reverent, one that makes you feel something akin to inspiration. . . .

Now, use this hymn as the place for your thoughts to go. Make it your emergency channel. Whenever you find that these shady actors have slipped from the sidelines of your thinking onto the stage of your mind, put on this record, as it were.

As the music begins and as the words form in your mind, the unworthy thoughts will slip shamefully away. The hymn will change the whole mood on the stage of your mind. Because it is uplifting and clean, the baser thoughts will disappear, for while virtue, by choice, *will not* associate with filth, evil *cannot* tolerate the presence of light. . . .

Once you learn to clear the stage of your mind from unworthy thoughts, keep it busy with learning worthwhile things. Change your environment so that you have things about you that will inspire good and uplifting thoughts. Keep busy with things that are righteous. (*Teach Ye Diligently* [Salt Lake City: Copyright Deseret Book Co., 1975], pp. 46–47. Used by permission.)

Truly, the best way to fight an evil thought is by preempting it with a wholesome one. We need not participate in a frontal contest between thoughts that are evil and thoughts that are good. We should fill the stage of our mind with what is good, and when this is done the doorkeeper of our minds will give no entrance to the evil, because there will be no vacancy in the place it seeks to occupy.

Reforming Our Motives

The eternal significance of action or inaction turns on the state of mind that motivated the act or omission. Acts that seem to be good bring blessings only when they are done with a good motive, with real and righteous intent.

We can work to reform our motives if we are continually asking ourselves: Why am I taking this action? That question is especially important for actions that we suppose to be good. It reminds us that it is not enough to act in ways that seem to be good. We must act for the right reasons. If we truly desire to please God and serve him, continual self-examination of our reasons for actions cannot fail to expose our selfish and sordid motives and challenge us to reform them.

The ultimate good motive for any act is charity—the pure love of Christ. We acquire that motive in two ways: (1) by praying for love, and (2) by practicing service.

We can affect our motives by prayer. The prophet Mormon gave the best teaching on how to use prayer to acquire the pure love of Christ:

> Wherefore, my beloved brethren, pray unto the Father with all the energy of heart, that ye may be filled with this love, which he hath bestowed upon all who are true followers of his Son, Jesus Christ; that ye may become the sons of God; that when he shall appear we shall be like him, for we shall see him as he is; that we may have this hope; that we may be purified even as he is pure (Moroni 7:48).

In order to learn to serve for the pure love of Christ, we must practice serving God and our fellowmen. Elder Marvin J. Ashton described the powerful influence of service: "We learn to love that which we serve, and we serve that which we love." He describes the effects of service on what we love:

> As adults, if our top priorities are constantly directed toward the acquisition of more and better worldly goods, it will not take long to increase our love in those directions. . . .
>
> How can we decrease our love for things not for our best good? We must . . . stop the expenditure of time and effort

148

By praying for charity and by practicing service, we can reform our motives and come to be filled with the pure love of Christ that is characteristic of the pure in heart.

---

in these directions. . . . Some callings and assignments in the Church may seem insignificant and unimportant at the time, but with each willingly fulfilled assignment, love of the Lord will grow. We learn to love God as we serve and know Him.

How can we help a new convert to learn to love the gospel? By finding ways for him to serve and sacrifice. We must constantly emphasize the truth that we love that to which we give time, whether it be the gospel, God, or gold. . . . Our appreciation and love of the gospel and its teachings will always be in proportion to our service and commitment to the gospel. (*Ye Are My Friends* [Salt Lake City: Deseret Book Co., 1982], pp. 13–14.)

By praying for charity and by practicing service, we can reform our motives and come to be filled with the pure love of Christ that is characteristic of the pure in heart.

Perfecting Our Desires

Our Heavenly Father knows the desires of our hearts and will judge us accordingly. He will punish evil desires and reward righteous ones.

We can suppress evil desires and substitute righteous ones. This involves education and practice. President Joseph F. Smith taught that the "education . . . of our desires is one of far-reaching importance to our happiness in life" (*Gospel Doctrine* [Salt Lake City: Deseret Book Co., 1919], p. 372).

I have sometimes heard a person say: "I hate him. I can't help how I feel." I have also heard someone say: "I can't stand to have anyone tell me what I must do. I can't help it. That's just the way I am." These assertions are mistaken. Feelings are subject to change. Our feelings are subject to our will.

Through our divinely granted willpower we have ultimate control over our desires. But the desires of our hearts are so deep-seated that it may take many years of practice for us to be sure that education and practice have perfected our desires to the point where all are entirely righteous.

Elder Joseph B. Wirthlin spoke of the process in these words:

> The springs of human action are inherently in the feelings, not the intellect. . . .
>
> Only in accepting our Savior and doing his will do we acquire the "feeling to do right." . . . Fundamental to most wrong-doing is a lack of desire. . . . Individuals who do right and "hunger and thirst after righteousness" (Matthew 5:6) get and keep alive through their actions the feeling to do right. Inherent in the first principles of the gospel is the "desire principle"—the desire to love God and fellowmen "with all thy heart, and with all thy soul, and with all thy mind." (Matthew 22:37.) ("There Am I in the Midst of Them," *Ensign*, May 1976, p. 56.)

We can begin the education of our desires by attempting to alter our feelings. The desires of our hearts are fundamental, but our feelings are closer to the surface and easier for us to identify and influence.

I have sometimes heard a person say: "I hate him. I can't help how I feel." I have also heard someone say: "I can't stand to have anyone tell me what I must do. I can't help it. That's just the way I am." These assertions are mistaken. Feelings *are* subject to change. Our feelings are subject to our will.

My widowed mother understood that principle. "Pray about your feelings," she used to say. She taught her three children to pray for the right kind of feelings about their experiences—positive or negative—and about the people they knew. If our feelings are good, we are more likely to have appropriate desires, to take right actions, and to act for the right reasons.

We can perfect our desires. God commands us to do so, and he will strengthen us in this effort if we will seek his help. President George Q. Cannon taught:

> No man ought to say, "Oh, I cannot help this; it is my nature." He is not justified in it, for the reason that God has promised to give strength to correct these things, and to give gifts that will eradicate them. If a man lack wisdom, it is his duty to ask God for wisdom. The same with everything else. That is the design of God concerning his Church. He wants his Saints to be perfected in the truth. For this purpose He gives these gifts, and bestows them upon those who seek after them, in order that they may be a perfect people upon the face of the earth. (*Millennial Star,* April 1894, pp. 260–61; quoted in *Doctrine and Covenants Student Manual,* 1981, p. 102.)

The Ultimate Reward

Modern revelation has reaffirmed the importance of being pure in heart:

> But blessed are the poor who are pure in heart, whose hearts are broken, and whose spirits are contrite, for they shall see the kingdom of God coming in power and great glory unto their deliverance; for the fatness of the earth shall be theirs (D&C 56:18).

Alma told the people of his day to imagine what it would be like to be brought before the tribunal of God. Then he asked:

> I say unto you, can ye look up to God at that day with a pure heart and clean hands? (Alma 5:19).

The Psalmist taught the same lesson:

> Who shall ascend into the hill of the Lord? or who shall stand in his holy place?
>
> He that hath clean hands, and a pure heart (Psalm 24:3–4).

Finally, Matthew 5:8 records our Savior's description of the ultimate reward:

"Blessed are the pure in heart: for they shall see God."

SUBJECT INDEX

Nephites, 79, 81, 143
cycles of righteousness and depravity,
105–9
laws of, 9
ministry of Christ among, 21, 22, 44,
108, 130
pride of, 97–98
priestcraft among, 40
New and everlasting covenant of
marriage, 70

– O –

Oaks, Dallin H., calling to Council of the
Twelve, 45
Obedience, 123, 127
"Oh Come, All Ye Faithful" (hymn),
128
Oppression, 67, 96, 110
Ordinances, 63, 69–71, 131–34
vicarious, 70–71
See also Baptism; Sacrament
"Our Spiritual Heritage" (speech), 117

– P –

Packer, Boyd K., on control of thoughts,
146–47
Teach Ye Diligently, 147
Parable, of the good Samaritan, 61, 78
of the great supper, 101–2
of the laborers in the vineyard, 139–40
of the Pharisee and the publican,
100–1
of the rich man and Lazarus, 63–64
of the sower, 54, 74
Parents, 117
"Parents' Concern for Children"
(speech), 35
Paul (the Apostle), 114
on charity, 23, 47, 57
on eternal perspective, 111–12
on God and Christ, 127
on the inner man, vii, 137
on judgment, 138
on the letter and the spirit, 15–16
on materialism, 77
on Moses, 118
on service, 43
on sorrow, 68
on thoughts, 6, 10
on a willing mind, 61
"thorn in the flesh" of, 67
Perfection, 138–39, 144

Perpetual Emigration Fund, 119
Perry, L. Tom, on pride, 95
"United in Building the Kingdom of
God," 95
Persecution, 5, 97, 105, 110, 122
"Personal Morality" (speech), 7
Personal Writings of Joseph Smith, The
(book), 5
Perspective, eternal, 111–12, 122
Peter (the Apostle), on pride, 109–10
on service, 39
on spirituality, 121
Petersen, Mark E., on hungering and
thirsting after righteousness, 69
on preparation for worship, 131
"The Sabbath Day," 131
Pharisees, 4, 10, 27, 100–101
Phelps, W. W., 5, 22
Pioneers, 118–19
Plan of salvation, 62
Podhoretz, Norman, "Candidates'
Morality Is Not Private," 91
Poor Richard's Almanac (book), 94
Pornography, 7, 98
Power, 73, 120
Pratt, Orson, on pride, 98
Prayer, 123, 128, 144, 148, 151
for witness of Book of Mormon, 19–20
on the sacrament, 132
with real intent, 23–25
Premortal life, of Christ, 135
Pride, 73, 89–110, 113, 121, 142
intellectual, 93–94
of comparison, 95–105, 108–10, 142–43
of self-satisfaction, 91–94, 104, 109,
142
Priestcraft, 16–18, 39–40
Priesthood, 102
righteous use of, 104
Priorities, 5–6, 51, 73–74, 77, 111, 120,
137–45
Prisons, 60
Prominence, 73, 75, 120
Promised Messiah, The (book), 127, 135
Prophecies, 44
Prophets, 124, 127
living, 123, 144
modern, 6, 81, 98
See also names of individual prophets
Prosperity, 75, 79, 83, 106
Publicans, 100–101
Punishment, fear of, 42
Purity of heart, means of attainment,
137–52

SCRIPTURE INDEX

OLD TESTAMENT

NEW TESTAMENT

BOOK OF MORMON

DOCTRINE AND COVENANTS

PEARL OF GREAT PRICE

Moses
1:6	127
1:17	125
1:39	136
2:28	87
3:3	27
5:5	125
6:65–66	70

Abraham
1:2	52

Joseph Smith–History
1:15	24
1:19	17